FROM ENGINEERING TO SALES

A sea of opportunities

GERMAN RUMINOT

From Engineering to Sales.

A sea of opportunities / German Ruminot

First edition, July 2023.
ISBN 978-956-414-740-6 (e-book)
ISBN 979-885-447-271-5

Dedicated to all those who are starting out in the world of sales.

Thank you, Victor Delgado for your contributions and reviews.

Table of Contents

Prologue

This work describes the process followed by the author to get started in the world of sales.

This book is based on real experiences of consultative sales, where detailed and rigorous sales processes must be carried out to achieve sales in highly competitive and changing markets.

All the analyses and proposals presented in this book are based on the author's real-world experiences and tests of sales processes with diverse customers in different countries.

This work also presents the reader with a plethora of terminology of concepts in the world of sales, introducing essential sales jargon used in this domain. The provided vocabulary will facilitate collaboration with peers and enable effective communication with all staff, directors, stakeholders, and other individuals within and outside the organization.

This is intended for readers who are interested in understanding and applying the sales process to their daily work. It serves as a practical guide, providing details on the sales process and real-life case analyses. Whether you're looking to learn the basics or review key concepts, this book is designed to meet your needs.

Introduction

Today, millions of dollars and hours are invested in training professionals from various industries to help them learn about the world of sales. The primary goal of such training is to generate and increase sales for businesses and companies.

The world of consultative sales is a dynamic and competitive world where professionals must cultivate discipline, perseverance, proactivity, and resilience to achieve the goal of a new sale.

This book serves as a practical guide, offering a range of proposals, analyses, examples, and recommendations to help achieve the first sale. Its purpose is to assist in the training of new professionals who are interested in entering the world of sales.

The opening chapters of this book outline the process for entering the world of sales, while the subsequent chapters delve into the step-by-step process for achieving the first sales. Closing the work with some conclusions and recommendations to improve the sales process.

From Engineering to Sales

Chapter 1: The Beginning of the Journey

The world of sales initially seemed distant and unfamiliar to me. I had limited exposure to how the commercial and marketing departments of a company managed the entire sales process. As a result, my understanding was mostly confined to the final stages, such as handling contracts, customer contacts, and implementing and supporting the products or services sold to new customers.

This way of working was my "comfort zone" for a long time. I was comfortably following my professional life as an engineer in the area of projects and services, until one day everything changed unexpectedly with a call from my boss who told me:

"...going forward, you will be responsible for managing the entire sales process, which means reaching out to potential customers and selling them our products and services prior to the start of any project".

After hearing that phrase, I said to myself: *What do I do now?* At first, I felt a bit frustrated and had the natural urge to give up, as I was unsure of how to handle this new situation. However, after taking some time to reflect, I decided to approach it as a new challenge and remain calm as I tackled it.

In the days that followed that episode, I continued to feel bewildered, as I lacked a fundamental understanding of sales. I experienced days of great uncertainty and unease, as I struggled to determine how best to embark on my new journey into the **world of sales**.

Having to leave my comfort zone as I was thrown into this new world. I began to investigate all the activities, concepts, processes, and new situations that I would have to address to achieve a sale. My initial reaction was to create an activity plan, similar to a project plan, that outlined all the necessary steps to achieve a sale within a specific timeframe. During this initial analysis, I was able to identify the following activities:

- o **Understand the market** in which I am going to sell.

- o **Search and select** future customers.

- o **Contact new customers** and arrange an initial meeting.

- o **Prepare and present your product** and/or service.

- o **Prepare a document with the proposed** solution.

- o **Negotiate the terms** of the sale of the product and/or service.

- o **Close and sign the agreement** (contract) of the sale.

As the months passed, I came to the realization that following all the steps and activities outlined in my general plan might not necessarily lead to generating new sales. I discovered that there were key elements missing from the process that I had not considered. From this initial analysis, I drew my first conclusion about sales:

"Unlike traditional engineering, sales processes cannot achieve the same results with 100% accuracy, as sales involves human interactions and is not based on a replicable scientific process."

This implied that the expected results of sales processes could not be systematically replicated for all customers in any market.

This realization prompted me to recognize the need to gain a more detailed understanding of all the factors and nuances that occur at each stage of the sales process. I realized that my initial analysis had likely overlooked critical details that couldn't be captured through a typical business plan.

During those days when I still could not close any sale, someone in the company where I worked told me the following:

"... Don't worry, when you sell your first product or service, the next sales will come by themselves."

From this phrase, I learned over time one of my first lessons on consultative sales:

"The sale of a product or service does not happen in a vacuum. There must be a prior effort to reach out to potential customers, showcase the product's attributes and benefits, and persuade them to acquire it. Whether it is the first or the last time that you offer products and/or services, the sales process must be applied to all potential customers."

So, in the following days and months, I dedicated myself to the complex task of structuring my own way of approaching the sales process using the new knowledge and the different experiences that I acquired over time.

In the upcoming chapters we will review all the steps, activities, experiences, and conclusions that I was making to achieve my first consultative sales. We will delve into the steps, activities, experiences, and conclusions that I gained during my journey towards achieving my first successful consultative sale.

Chapter 2: Sales Process

After overcoming my initial shock and confusion, I embraced sales as a new world for me. I recognized the importance of organizing my thoughts and grasping the fundamental concepts in this field. I was now determined to define a clear process that would lead me to achieve my goal of **"making a sale"**.

Sales concepts

To gain a foothold in the world of sales, I needed to familiarize myself with key concepts and terminology. These are some of the most used:

o *Business to Business (B2B)*: This corresponds to sales that occur between two companies or businesses. This can include the sale of services such as accounting or marketing. This book focuses on analyzing and providing examples within the B2B sales context.

- o *Business-to-consumer (B2C)*: This involves selling products or services directly to the end consumer. Examples include selling shoes or clothes directly to customers through a retail store or e-commerce website.

- o *Market Segment:* It is a group of customers and consumers with a set of common characteristics and needs.

- o *Niche Market:* This is a subset of a larger market that caters to a specific customer group with distinct needs or preferences. It may not have many customers, but it can provide significant opportunities for companies that specialize in serving it.

- o *Prospecting:* This relates to the process of finding potential customers or leads for a business.

- o *Cold call:* This is the act of making unsolicited calls to a potential customer without any prior communication or relationship, with the aim of scheduling a first meeting or to make a sales pitch.

o *Lead:* This concept represents a potential customer whose contact information we have, but who has not yet expressed any intention to purchase, therefore not yet qualified as a Prospect.

o *Prospect:* This term refers to a potential customer who is likely to make a purchase but has not yet made a final decision to buy the product or service.

o *Client:* This refers to a prospect who has signed a contract to purchase a product or service. At that precise moment, they have become a customer.

These concepts can be summarized in the following scheme:

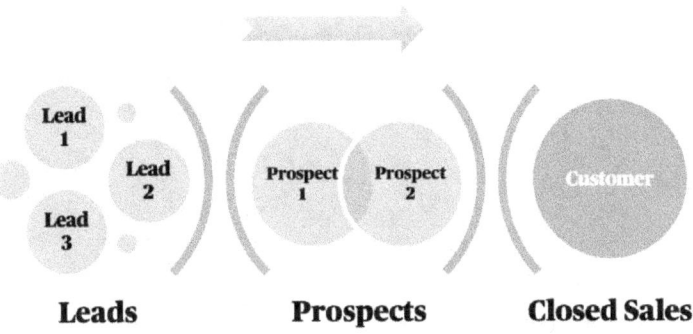

Figure 1 Leads, prospects and customers.

o *Future customer*: In this book we will use the concept of the future customer to refer indistinctly to a potential customer (lead) or prospect.

o Pipeline: This is a list of potential customers and prospects that are currently in the sales process, starting from the initial contact and moving towards closing the sale. The pipeline can be visualized as a funnel, as there are typically many prospects at the top, but only a few will ultimately become customers.

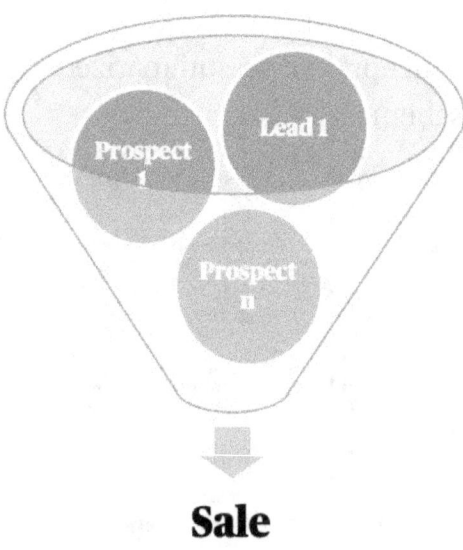

Figure 2 Sales funnel

o *Master Service Agreement (MSA)*: It is a framework contract that defines the conditions of your future transactions and service agreement between the client and the supplier.

o *Service Level Agreement (SLA)*: This defines the level of service required by the customer from the supplier for a particular product or service. This agreement may be included in the contract signed between the parties for the purchase of the product and / or service.

o *Market Share*: This concept refers to the partition of a company's sales from the market and is calculated by dividing the company's sales from the total market sales over a specific period, such as annually or semi-annually.

o *Share of wallet (SOW)*: This concept is used in marketing to indicate the portion of a customer's expenses that a company captures. In simple terms, it is defined as the percentage of a customer's total spending in a particular market that goes to a specific company over a certain period of time. For example, if a customer spends $100 on various food products in a week and only $10 on bread, then the share of wallet for the bread company is calculated as 10/100 = 10% of that customer's spending for the week.

o *Statement of work (SOW)*: A document that describes the requirements of the Project, for the service or product to be contracted.

o *Conversion Rate*: This term is used to describe the probability of completing the sale based on the total number of leads in your funnel.

o *Sales Forecast*: This concept refers to the estimation of sales that a company or business expects to achieve for a given period, such as quarterly, biannually, or annually.

o *Sales quota*: This is the sales target set by a company for a specific period, such as quarterly, bi-annually, or annually, which is then assigned to individual sales representatives.

o *Up-selling*: It is the practice of offering a customer a higher-quality or premium product, service, or feature with the aim of increasing revenue.

o *Cross selling:* It is the practice of offering a complementary product or service to a customer who has already purchased or is in the process of purchasing another product.

o *Bonus for sale:* It refers to a benefit, usually a monetary incentive, offered by a company to a salesperson for achieving a specific sales target or quota within a designated period, such as quarterly, semi-annually, or annually.

o *Customer relationship management (CRM) system:* This is a tool that enables businesses to manage customer interactions and relationships throughout the sales, marketing, and after-sales service process.

o *Sponsor:* A person or entity, inside or outside the company, who advocates for a product or service and promotes its purchase to others. The sponsor can provide valuable support in directing actions within the company and assisting in negotiations to close a sale.

o *Partner:* A business partner who helps you with marketing and product or service sales.

- o *Demo:* It refers to the process of making a presentation of the functionality and benefits of the product and / or service to future customers.

- o *Pilot*: It refers to performing a test with customer data in a sector or a certain area to show the benefits and functionalities of the product and / or service.

- o *Objections:* This concept corresponds to the concerns and challenges that prospects raise, hindering the advancement in the sales process.

- o *Proof of Concept (PoC):* It refers to a test that seeks to prove the technical feasibility of a client's idea or project using the functionalities of the product and/or service to be sold.

The general sales process

After understanding the basic terminology about sales, the first thing I thought about was to analyze and define a *General Sales Process*. I wanted to be able to capture in one place all the variables, inputs, activities, processes, and outputs that it should contain to achieve a consultative sale.

My objective was to use this process as my guide to lead prospects from the initial activity to the final stage of making a purchase and transitioning them into becoming satisfied customers.

Activities and aspects of the process

To define this process, it was first necessary to analyze all the aspects and activities that were key to the success of the sale. According to my initial explorations, the key elements to consider were:

- The **target market.**
- **Future customers** (Leads and Prospects)
- **Tools to sell.**
- **Value proposal** (of the product and/or service).
- The **technical and economic offer.**
- The **negotiation.**
- The **closing** of the sale.

Among the main activities to reach the goal of the sale were:

- Exploring and understanding the Target Market.

- The factors that influence the definition of purchase.
- Regulators or government entities that regulate the market.
- The sales process of that market.
- Stationary factors affecting the purchase.
- The customer buying cycle.

- Size of the Target Market.

  - Sales volumes.
  - Purchase volumes.
  - Market growth in recent years and future projections.

- Key Market Leaders.

  - Determine and classify key market players.
    - Market leaders (customers).
    - Market innovators.
    - Competitors.
    - Regulators.
    - Complementary companies that could help enter the market.

- Future Customers

    o Total market or the future customers to contact.
    o List of Leads and Prospects (Possible customers).
    o Current customers.
    o Categorize future customers based on their willingness to buy.

- Sale Tools

    o Marketing strategy (price, point of sale, product, promotion).
    o Brochures, demos, pilots, meetings, etc.

- Value Proposal

    o Benefits obtained using the product and / or service.
    o Key functionalities of the product and/or service that differentiate you from the rest.

- Commercial Offer

- o Economic proposal of the service and / or product.

- Negotiation
  - o Sale closing negotiations.
  - o Types of contracts.

- Closing of the sale
  - o Signing of the contract.

Process overview

After reviewing and analyzing all the information gathered in the existing sales literature and from conversations with experienced salespeople. I will delve into the fundamental topics that are crucial to understanding the journey towards achieving a consultative sale.

Next, I will provide a general outline of the process that I have designed based on all the analyses mentioned. This scheme is divided into eight specific steps, each with measurable and expected results. By focusing on achieving the desired outcomes at each step, I significantly increased my probability of closing the sale.

Step 1: *Market Analysis*
Objective

· Understanding the market
· Sizing the market

Step 2: Prospect

· New customers (leads, prospects)
· Current customers

Step 3: Preparing the sale

· Presentations
· Demos
· Pilots

Step 4: Generate a Value proposal

· Benefits
· Key functionalities

Step 5: Negotiate

· Jumping obstacles
· Contracts

Step 6: Monitoring and Controlling

· Actions to move forward

Step 8: Process retrospective

• Agility in the process
• Simplicity of the process
• Areas for improvement
• Highlights of the process

Step 7: Closing the sale

· Signing of contract
· Start of service

Figure 3 The sales process

Analysis of the sales process

Next, I devoted myself to conducting a comprehensive review of each input and output of the steps in the general sales process. I have provided a detailed breakdown of these steps below.

Step 1: Market analysis objective

In this step of the process, it is important to consider the following inputs and outputs for target market analysis:

- **Inputs**
  - Fairs, Exhibitions, Events, social media.
  - Industry Magazines and Websites.
  - Market buying process.
  - Customer purchase volumes.
  - Market sales volumes.

- **Outputs**
  - Analysis of competitors and partners.
  - Market shares of the product or service.
  - Target market map.
  - List of future customers in the market.

Graphically the analysis would look like this:

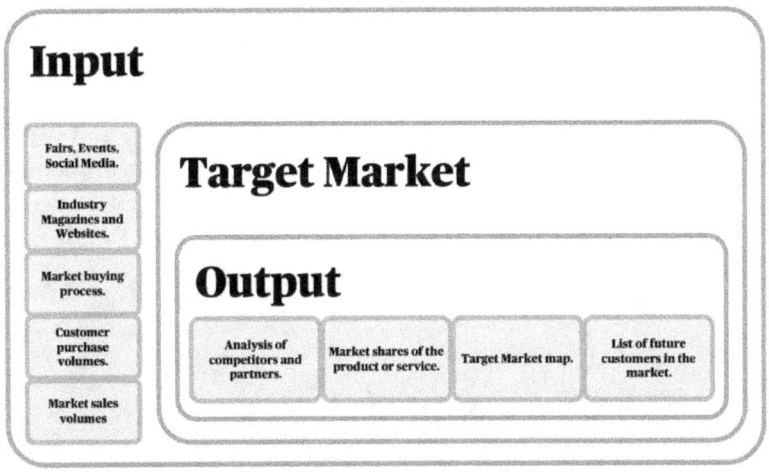

Figure 4 Inputs and outputs of the market objective analysis

Step 2: Prospect

In this step of the process, it is essential to use the previous market analysis as inputs for prospecting:

- o **Inputs**
  - Market shares of the product or service.
  - Target Market map.
  - List of future customers in the market.

- o **Outputs**
  - Create categorization of future customers.
  - Prioritization of new prospects.
  - Current situation (economical, political, etc.) of customers.
  - List of future customers in the market.

25

- First contacts.

Graphically it would look like this:

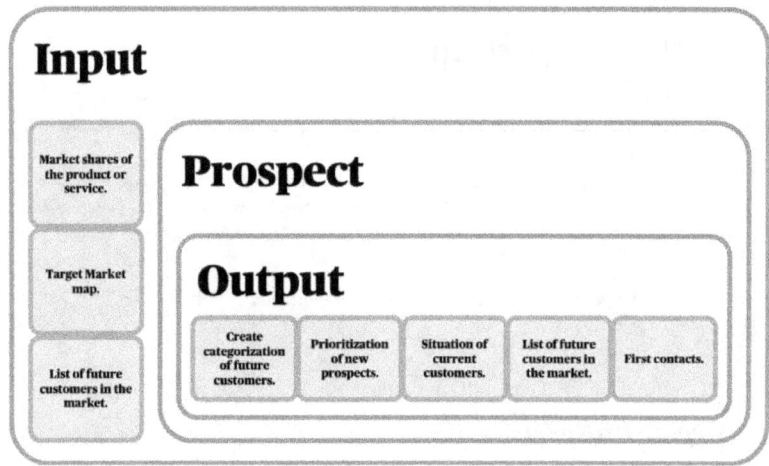

Figure 5 Inputs and outputs for prospecting

Step 3: Preparing the sale.

Preparing the sale is a crucial step in the process, as it enables you to showcase the unique benefits and advantages of your product in solving the problem, distinguishing it from others in the market:

- o **Inputs**
  - Future customers to contact.
  - Initial needs and problems.
  - Identify the meeting audience.

- Features and benefits of the product or service to be sold.

o **Outputs**
   - Stakeholders map.
   - Prepare the sales script.
   - Tell a story in reference to the product or service.
   - Demonstrations.
   - Presentations.
   - Success story.
   - Pilot.

Graphically it would look like this:

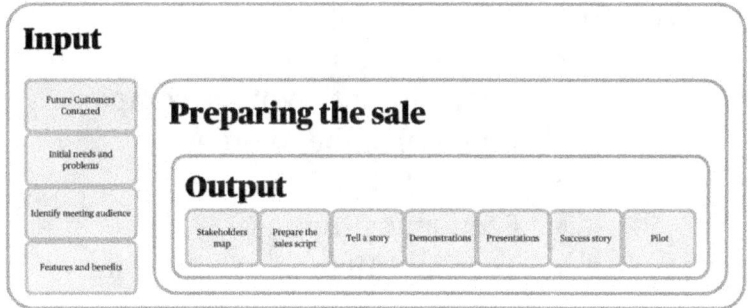

Figure 6 Inputs and outputs when preparing the sale.

Step 4: Generate a value proposal.

In this step of the process, we aim to create a compelling proposal that persuades and convinces the prospective customer to proceed with the purchase. Thus, the content of the proposal plays a pivotal role:

- o **Inputs**
    - Core challenges and requirements.
    - Deadlines to deliver the proposal and the product.
    - Sponsor Impressions.
    - Impressions of presentations, pilots, PoC, and customer demos.

- o **Outputs**
    - Executive Summary.
    - Brief description of the company.
    - Proposal of the solution.
    - Detail of benefits.
    - Economic proposal.
    - Type and Method of payment.
    - Details of possible benefits.
    - Time of validity of the proposal.
    - Success stories.

Graphically it would look like this:

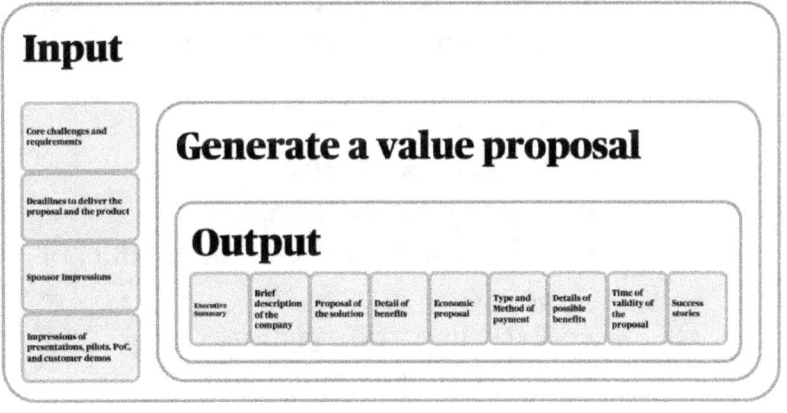

77 Inputs and outputs to generate a sales proposal.

Step 5: Negotiate

This step is the final one before closing the sales process and can often be the most extensive and complex, as it involves completing the sale:

- **Inputs**
  - Price of the product or service.
  - Additional functionality for the case of products.
  - Scope of services (territorial, functional, etc.).
  - Duration of the contract.
  - Installation deadlines.
  - Service start dates or product usage.
  - Type and form of payments.
  - Payment currency.
  - Volume discount
  - Exclusivity of use.
  - Brand reproduction.
  - Advertising for use of the product or service.
  - Early departure clauses.
  - Fines for non-compliance.
  - Agreement Frameworks and Specific Service Levels. (SLA, MSA)

- **Outputs**
  - Management of all objections.
  - Negotiations.
  - Objections Follow-up.

- Contract agreement.

Graphically it would look like this:

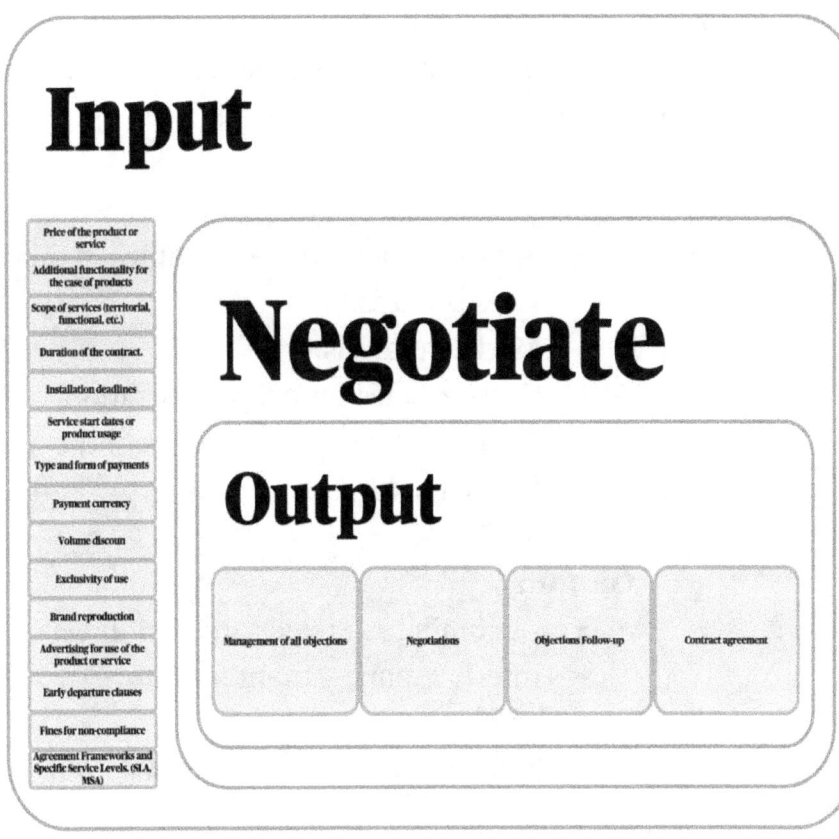

Figure 8 Inputs and outputs of the negotiation.

Step 6: Monitoring and controlling.

In this step of the process, it is key to use the previous market analysis, sales preparation, value proposition, and ongoing negotiations as inputs to analyze each prospect in the process:

- o **Inputs**
    - Status of each future customer in the sales process.
    - Market analysis.
    - Current sales funnel prioritization.
    - Actions taken and responses of the future customer.

- o **Outputs**
    - Upcoming strategies and actions.
    - Internal management for future actions.
    - New prioritization of the sales funnel.

Graphically it would look like this:

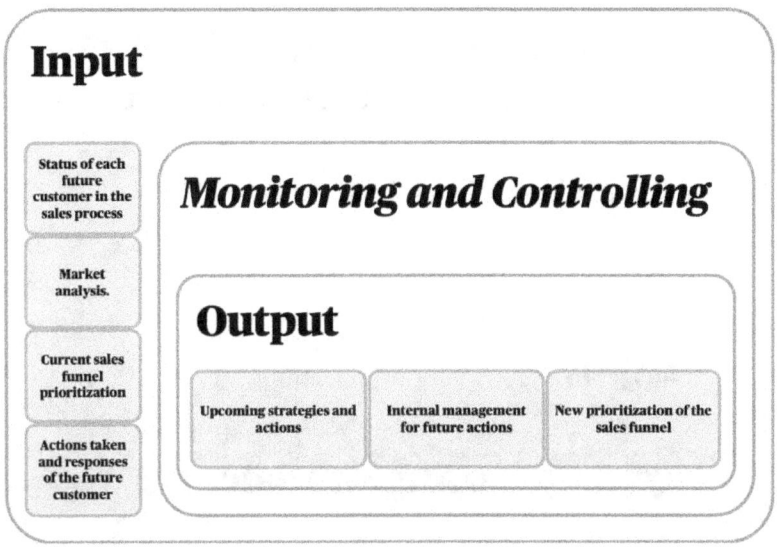

Figure 9 Inputs and outputs for monitoring and controlling.

Step 7: Closing the sale.

In this step of the process, the objective is to formalize all the negotiations in an agreement or contract to finalize the sale formally:

- o **Inputs**
  - Contract Agreement.
  - Contract.
  - Service start date or use of the product.

- o **Outputs**

- Signing the contract.
- Start of service or use of the product.

Graphically it would look like this:

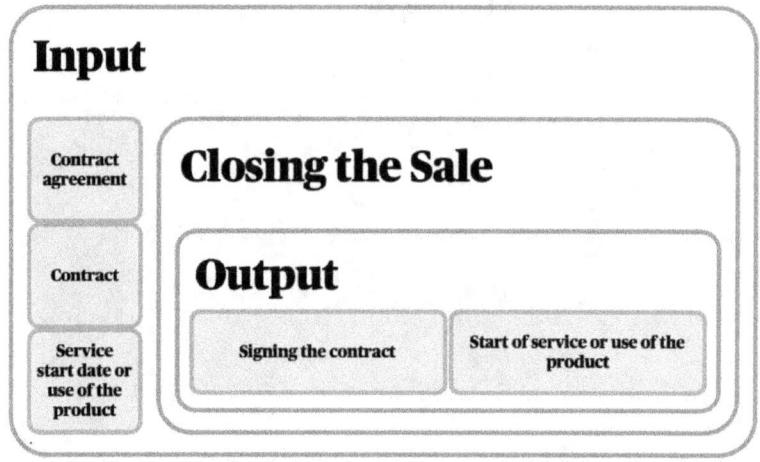

Figure 10 Inputs and outputs to close the sale.

Step 8: Retrospective of the process

The objective of this step is to analyze the positive aspects, customer impressions, and areas for improvement in your sales process. This step is especially relevant when you are just starting in the sales role, as it allows you to refine your process for future customers and successfully close the sale:

- o **Inputs**
  - Internal analysis of the selling process.
  - Agility in the process.
  - Simplicity of the process.
  - Topics for improvement.
  - Highlights of the process.

- o **Outputs**
  - Process improvement proposals.

Graphically it would look like this:

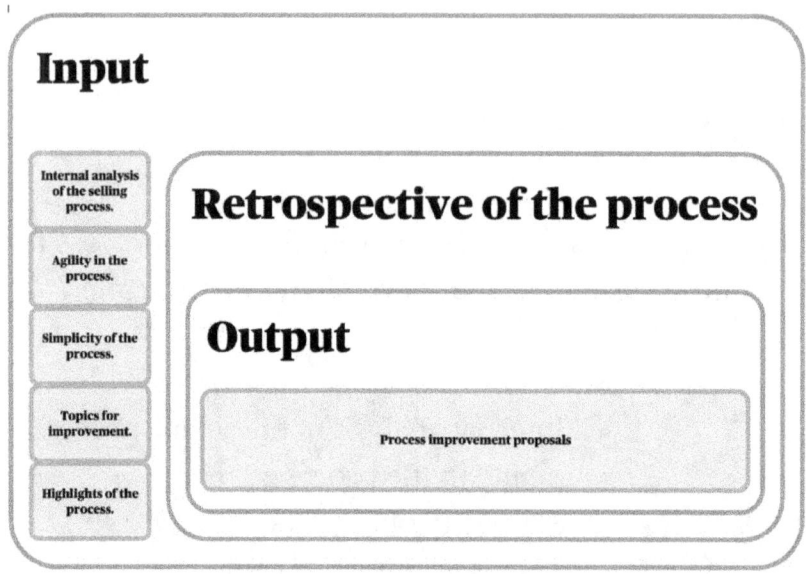

Figure 11 Retrospective of the process

Understanding the product and service

After defining the sales process, I set myself the task of understanding the product and service in detail that needs to be sold. This step is essential to initiate the sales process successfully. Among the topics that we need to know are:

o Understand the product/service thoroughly, in other words, the problems or needs it addresses.

o The key and differentiating functionalities with respect to competitors.

o What extraordinary or atypical features does the product or service offer to customers?

o What are the monetary and non-monetary benefits that can be obtained with the use of the product or service?

o How long does it take to obtain the benefits?

o What is the marketing strategy of the product or service, requirements for its use, implementation, prices, discounts, promotions, guarantees, after-sales services, etc.?

o At this stage it is important to review and analyze a demonstration of the product and/or service, in particular:

- o Key functionalities that allow you to achieve the benefits.
- o Functional differentiators with respect to the competition.
- o New features that do not exist in the market.
- o Specific functionalities for certain types of users.

- o Analyze success stories of current customers, reviewing in particular:

  - o Benefits obtained by the customer.
  - o Project Times and Risks.
  - o Implemented Decisions.
  - o Sales prices.

At the end of this analysis, you must be able to know what your product and / or service does, the benefits that can be obtained and that differentiate it from other competitors in the market. By understanding these concepts, you can effectively initiate the sales processes and ensure its success.

Furthermore, it is crucial to maintain a strong conviction and motivation in promoting the positive aspects of your product or service, while also acknowledging and addressing any weaknesses or limitations. This mindset will propel you forward in the sales process.

Key elements for the sales process.

After many iterations with different sales processes, I noticed that there are key elements necessary to successfully move forward and close a consultative sale. The items I identified were:

- o Understand the prospect's core problem and need.

- o Generate value to your future customer with your solution detailing the benefits achieved in justifying the purchase.

- o Generate the synergy so that the prospect trusts you, the product, and the company you represent.

- o Prepare rebuttals for objections.

o   After accomplishing all of the above, then call
    to action to close the deal.

Each of these topics will be reviewed in detail
in the next chapters.

Chapter 3: Analysis of the Target Market

U nderstanding the target market is the first step in the world of sales and is the basis of the overall sales process. Therefore, it is important to understand how the market where we want to perform the sales process works.

Understanding the target market

After gaining clarity on the product or service I intended to sell, I embarked on understanding the target market. This involved comprehensively identifying and analyzing all the actors within the market and understanding how they move and interact within the ecosystem.

To exemplify what needs to be determined at this point, let us take a country's solar energy sector.

To sell a product or service in this market, we must find out in different sources such as websites of the sector, networks, specialized groups, magazines, social media, etc., the following points:

- o Which companies are in the solar energy generation sector and what is their participation?

- o Which companies in the solar energy sector invest the most in new products and/or services?

- o What is their purchasing process? Is it direct purchase? Is it based in obtaining three quotes from different vendors and the most economical offer wins? Or do they typically require a tender to acquire a product or service?

- o For companies in this sector, who makes the purchasing decision? The owner, the board, the general manager, a procurement department, the operations manager, etc.?

- o Who uses the services and products I sell? Will this person be our gateway to demonstrate or generate the need?

- o Who are the suppliers in the sector?

- o Who is the leader or reference in sales and services?

- o What is the revenue volume driving the solar energy market in the country?

- o What is the role of the state in the market, for example, in terms of regulation and subsidies?

- o Does the state regulate the market and determine prices, market shares or percentages of investment in new products or innovation in the sector?

- o Are there any new projects in the portfolio regulated for tender or acquisition in the short, medium, and long term?

- o How do customers buy? For example: on credit, cash, license purchasing, services, SaaS, leasing, etc.

To explain how markets vary depending on country and culture, we take the software sales market in Brazil as an example and compare it to the software sales market in the Middle East:

- o In Brazil, companies generally prefer to buy software in SaaS mode and local currency.

- o In Middle East where they have greater purchasing power it is possible to sell software licenses in US dollars or euros.

The previous example clearly demonstrates the importance of understanding the market and its purchasing process in the target area where you intend to sell your product or service.

Sources of information

To get market detail I started to explore different sources of information, such as data from the marketing, sales, and commercial departments of my company, as well as social networks, specialized magazines, industry databases, etc.

Additionally, to obtain more information about the market, it is highly recommended to participate in seminars, symposiums, conferences, events, and all kinds of activities where your potential customers attend and participate.

You would be surprised of the many opportunities you obtain from:

- o Market information.
- o Suppliers.

- o Potential Customers.
- o New contacts.
- o Generate upcoming meetings.
- o Etc.

Furthermore, during breaks and work groups at these events, it is important to engage in conversations with as many attendees as possible to foster synergies and gather valuable information.

From my experience, these types of events are highly valuable for establishing your presence and promoting your product or service. They provide an excellent opportunity to generate a substantial number of contacts, which can significantly propel your progress in the sales process.

One of the significant insights I gained from attending these events is that every market has its unique codes, terminologies, key concepts, and purchasing processes. It is crucial to thoroughly understand and grasp these aspects to effectively sell within that market.

Additionally, it can be concluded that market analysis is specific to each country and culture in which you want to sell. These factors directly influence how your future customers buy, interact, and how sales are conducted within the sector.

Purchasing process

A relevant aspect to understand within market analysis is the buying process of your target market, which involves deciphering aspects such as:

- o *Which product or services* do they buy?

- o *When do they buy?* (Summer, at the beginning of the year, at Christmas, etc.)

- o *How often?* (Twice a year, recurring monthly, etc.)

- o *The activities and duration* of each stage of the purchase process.

What we seek to understand is the purchase process with the different activities that are needed to complete the entire process. For example, a potential customer in a mature market may need to:

1. **Define** the need for the product or service.

2. **Analyze the** different products and / or services in the market.

3. **Request initial** quotes from different suppliers.

4. **Raise internal budget** to cover the need.

5. **Evaluate** the proposals.

6. **Make the decision** to buy.

7. **Close** the purchase.

Each stage of the purchase process has a certain duration, considering the time from when the need is identified until the product or service is acquired. For example, in private companies, this process can take around six months, while in public companies or government entities, it may extend to one or two years. However, it's important to note that the duration can vary depending on the country and market dynamics.

Here is a graphic example of a purchase process.

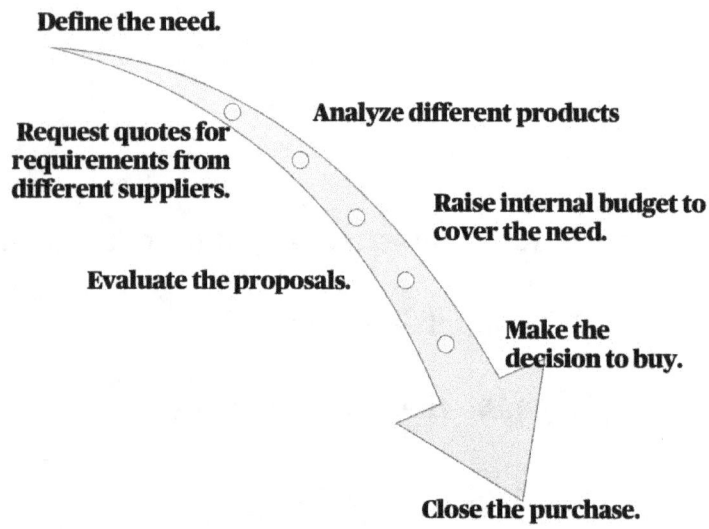

Define the need.

Analyze different products

Request quotes for requirements from different suppliers.

Raise internal budget to cover the need.

Evaluate the proposals.

Make the decision to buy.

Close the purchase.

Figure 12 The purchasing cycle

Volume of purchases

Continuing the market analysis, gathering information on market purchase volume is crucial to understand market demand and customer buying patterns. This data can be obtained through internal analysis, interviews, social media, surveys, industry publications, market studies, and public company reports.

The first essential step in analyzing this data is to validate the type of product or service your future customers are buying and understanding their buying behavior. Additionally, it's crucial to determine the current purchase volume within the sector.

This analysis will help identify market leaders and followers, enabling you to understand your future customers and adapt your strategies accordingly. It also provides insights into the competitive landscape and helps you position your product or service effectively in the target market.

The following diagram shows an example of a market with its purchase volume.

Market buyers

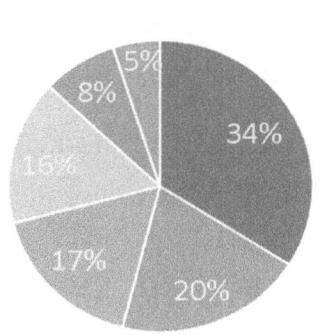

■ Customer 1 ■ Customer 2 ■ Customer 3 ■ Customer 4 ■ Customer 5 ■ Customer 6

Figure 13 Market buyers

49

Volume of sales

Continuing the market analysis, understanding the market's sales volume is also essential. This data reveals the market's supply distribution among various players and provides insights into how competitors are positioned. By obtaining this information, you can better understand your target market and its competitive landscape.

The goal of analyzing this data is to increase the sales volume of the market or capture a position in it.

Market share

Once you have the overall sales volume data of the market, it is important to analyze the market share of each player to determine their respective positions.

This allows you to assess your company's current standing within the market and understand its level of market penetration compared to competitors.

The following diagram shows an example of the Sales Market Share

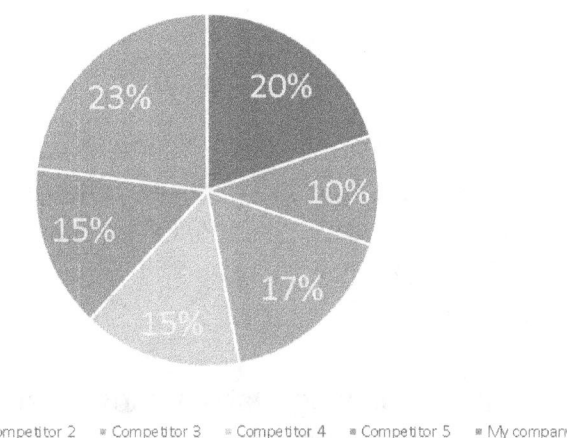

Figure 14 Sales market share

Analysis of competitors

As part of the market analysis, it is key to identify and analyze your competitors. Understanding who your competitors are and their strategies for market positioning is of utmost importance. This includes evaluating their differentiation strategies in comparison to your product or service, as well as assessing their strengths and weaknesses.

To stay well-informed and gather as much information as possible, it's important to actively engage in various sources such as websites, seminars, events, customer interactions, and more. By doing so, you can identify the market leaders, followers, and their respective market shares, which may change over time.

The following table shows an example of competitor analysis considering the following variables:

- o **Customers**.
- o **Strengths** of the product or service you offer.
- o **Weaknesses**
- o **Competitive advantage** over other market players
- o **Prices** offered by the market.
- o **Diversification** of your products and/or services
- o **Partners and suppliers**.

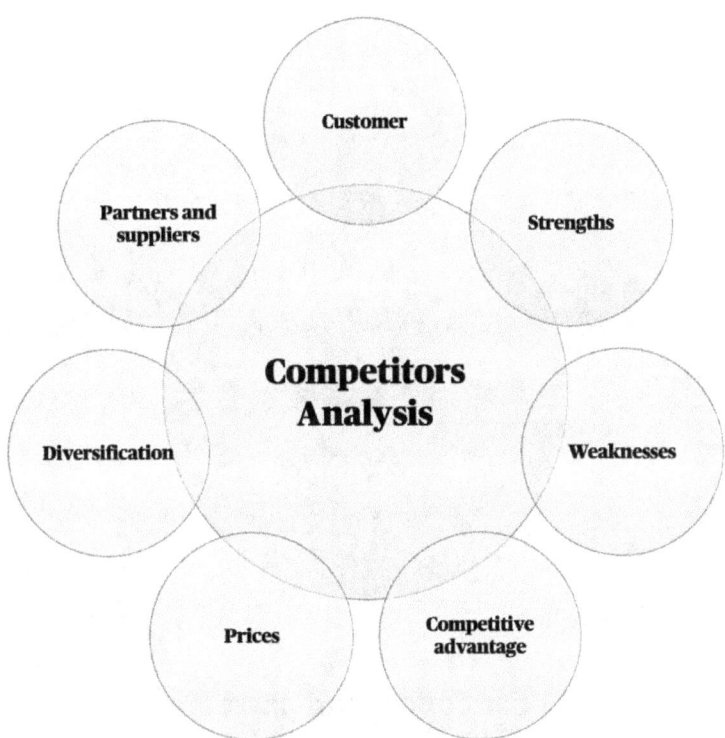

Figure 15 Analysis of competitors

Additionally, you can create a detailed analysis of the competitors which will allow you to track all variables, such as the ones shown below:

Analysis	Competitor SS	Competitor HH
Customer	Company A and Company B (market leader)	Company R and Company Athena
Strengths	Fast product installation and service support excellence	German brand and product reliability
Weaknesses	Limited base functionality the rest is added on a custom basis	Support only during European hours
Competitive advantage	Most innovative and market leader	Highest quality and reliable product over time
Prices	Highest price	Average market price
Diversification	Several complementary products	It has only two products
Partners and suppliers	Company HY	Comany JH and Hort

Figure 16 Detailed competitor analysis

Analysis of suppliers and partners

As part of the market analysis, it is important to characterize the various suppliers operating in the market. By doing so, you can identify strategic and key players who can potentially assist you in the sales process. Among these suppliers, you may even find potential partners who can collaborate with you in selling your products or services. Building partnerships with such suppliers can provide valuable support, resources, and expertise to enhance your sales efforts and expand your market reach.

Furthermore, as you analyze the market and its suppliers, you may identify potential synergies with certain suppliers that could transform into strategic partnerships. These partnerships can be based on the value proposition you offer to the market, where your products or services complement each other.

New product in target market

In certain cases, when entering an economic sector with a new product or service without a sales history, a clearly defined market objective may not exist. In such situations, you must exert extra effort to create the need in the market. The challenge lies in making potential customers envision the need your product addresses and convincingly demonstrate how your product fulfills these new needs with its unique benefits.

For new products and services without a sales history, we need to identify and focus efforts on innovative customers, often referred to as *"early adopters"*. These customers are more open to trying out new and innovative offerings and are willing to embrace the benefits of cutting-edge solutions.

Another way to reach out to a market without a sales history, is seeking out strategic partners and suppliers who can vouch for your product or service and help you connect with potential customers by leveraging through their existing networks and credibility.

If you manage to convince this part of the market, you can become the leader of the incipient market, generating important economic benefits, but always taking into consideration that this process of convincing the market to buy your new product can take an important time and a lot of economic effort. It will be key to determine the innovative companies in the sector, which are pioneers in adapting new innovations and products to be able to move forward.

In this scenario, as mentioned earlier, the selling process can indeed be more extensive in terms of time and resources compared to a mature market with an established sales history.

Resilience and persistence are key words that you must embody in this type of market. The main objective in this period is to gain recognition and generate a significant number of prospects for presentations, demonstrations, and pilots. This approach aims to secure future customers who are willing to try and adopt your product or service.

Target market map

After having analyzed all these aspects about the target market, I was able to define a target market map in which I wanted to sell.

Below is an example of the Target Market Map, which helped me understand the composition of the market and how these various actors interacted within the ecosystem:

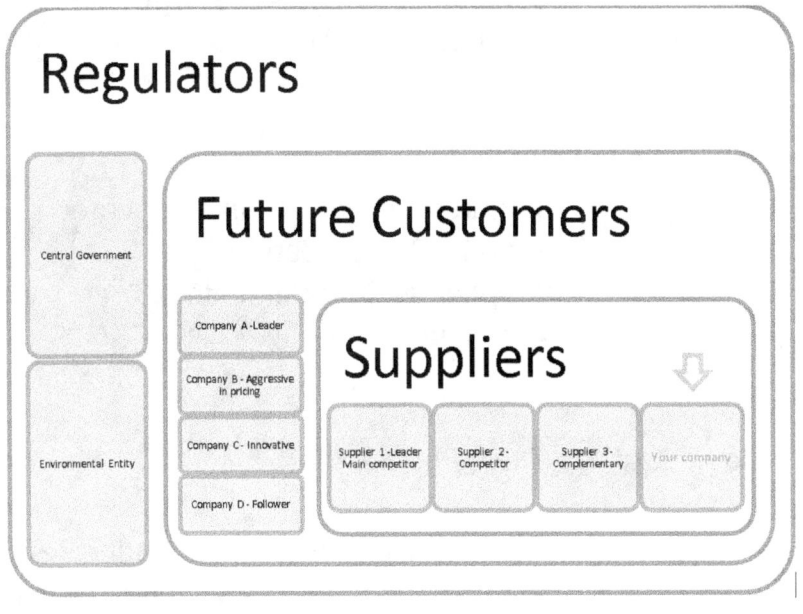

Figure 17 Target market map

This scheme provides a clear vision of the Target Market and your position as a sales company within it. It enables you to analyze the areas of this market where you can strategically focus your sales efforts to maximize results.

- Regulators
    - Central Government
    - Environmental Entity

- Future Customers
    - Company A -Leader
    - Company B - Aggressive in pricing
    - Company C - Innovative
    - Company D - Follower

- Suppliers
    - Supplier 1 -Leader Main competitor
    - Supplier 2 - Competitor
    - Supplier 3 - Complementary
    - *Your company*

Tracking the target market

One topic I have learned over time about sales is that tracking the target market is a truly relevant topic, as it directly affects the dynamics of your sales process. The question I asked myself at the time was:

Why do I need to track the target market?

o *The target market is dynamic* changing its needs, actors, and regulations so tracking is key to maintaining or increasing its positioning in this.

o *Changes from the regulator that affect the market*: It can impact regulations on new products, customers, and the market in general, consequently this can generate new sales opportunities or threats to your products or services.

o *Customer merger:* It can affect the sale of products or generate new needs.

o New competitors: It can impact the composition of the market, if they incorporate new technologies, new prices, or services.

o *Merger of competitors:* It can generate economies of scale and more competition with other market players.

o *New projects or customers in the market*: it can generate new sales opportunities in general.

o *New suppliers:* The entry of a new supplier can help improve your service and/or product.

o *Equipment changes within prospects or existing customer companies:* These changes create opportunities to showcase your products and/or services to potential new customers. For existing clients, it's important to assess if there are any new needs or changes in requirements due to these equipment changes.

The information for market monitoring can be obtained from the websites of the sector, contact networks, specialized groups, magazines, seminars, events, social media, etc.

Finally, it is important to note that the frequency of market monitoring can vary, ranging from biweekly to semi-annually. The chosen frequency should align with the pace of market evolution and dynamics within your specific sector.

Chapter 4: Prospecting

After conducting a detailed analysis of the market and gaining a thorough understanding of how it operates, the next step is prospecting. Prospecting involves creating a list of potential customers in order of priority and with the purpose of contacting them to offer your product and/or service.

What is prospecting?

This was the initial question that arose when I started focusing on this stage of the process. In simple terms, prospecting is the act of actively searching for potential customers who are likely to make a purchase.

Note: *According to surveys conducted among sellers, prospecting is often considered one of the most important and challenging activities in the sales process, second only to the closing stage, which involves converting prospects into actual customers.*

Prospect characterization

Before reaching out to potential prospects, it is indeed beneficial to define a profile that represents the type of customer you aim to persuade to purchase your product or service. In doing so, the following concepts should be considered:

- o Does the company prefer to use new technology?
- o Is it innovative?
- o Does it have coverage in several territories?
- o What is its market share?
- o Does the company take business risk?
- o Is the contact a decision maker?
- o Is the company in the target market?
- o Etc.

This characterization process will be tailored to the unique product or service you are selling, and it will evolve as you progress through the sales process and encounter new customer profiles. However, it serves as an initial step in identifying and targeting your future customers.

After achieving this first characterization, I thought about prioritizing the list of future customers, based on certain characteristics that suited the type of client I was looking for.

Next, we will review a list of attributes that are considered relevant in profiling and prioritizing prospects:

1818 Example of prospect profiling

The prospect market.

A first factor to consider when prioritizing prospects is their market share (indicator 1 to 100).

We may have prospects who have significant participation locally, but low regionally or globally.

Categorization

Categorization is a second factor to consider for prioritizing your future customers. The objective of this activity is to define the type of client. Categorization can consider the following forms of a future customer:

- o **Market leader (4):** This category dominates the market and looks for products that allow them to improve their leadership.

- o **Innovative (3):** These types of customers are those who are willing to introduce innovative products and services to their companies.

- o **Follower (2):** This type of customer copies the already proven ideas of the leader and innovator and implements them in their company.

- o **Conservative (1):** This category of customer requires all the necessary presentations, pilots, and demonstrations to convince them to introduce your product in their company. They may have the longest sales process.

Note: *The value assigned for each categorization in the prioritization process is indicated in parentheses.*

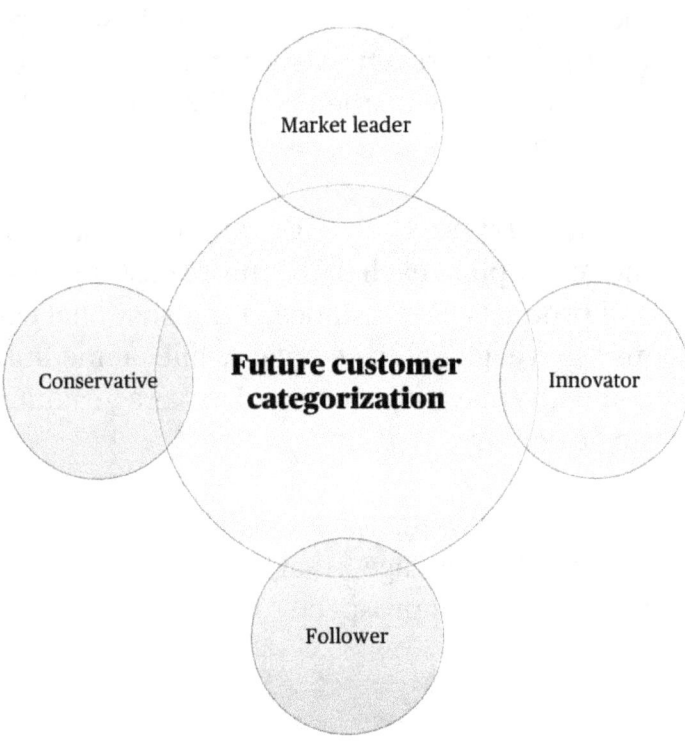

Figure 19 Analysis of future customer

Territorial coverage

Another important consideration in prioritizing potential customers is their territorial coverage, which refers to the extent of their operations in terms of services and products.

Assessing how your product or service will impact the prospect's territory upon purchase helps tailor your sales approach, demonstrate value, and align your offering with their specific needs and market requirements.

The *territorial coverage* can be defined based on the geographic reach of the future customer's services and products. For instance, a transnational company may have global coverage, while a medium-sized company may have national coverage limited to a single country.

The following diagram shows the types of territorial coverage that we could find when characterizing a prospect:

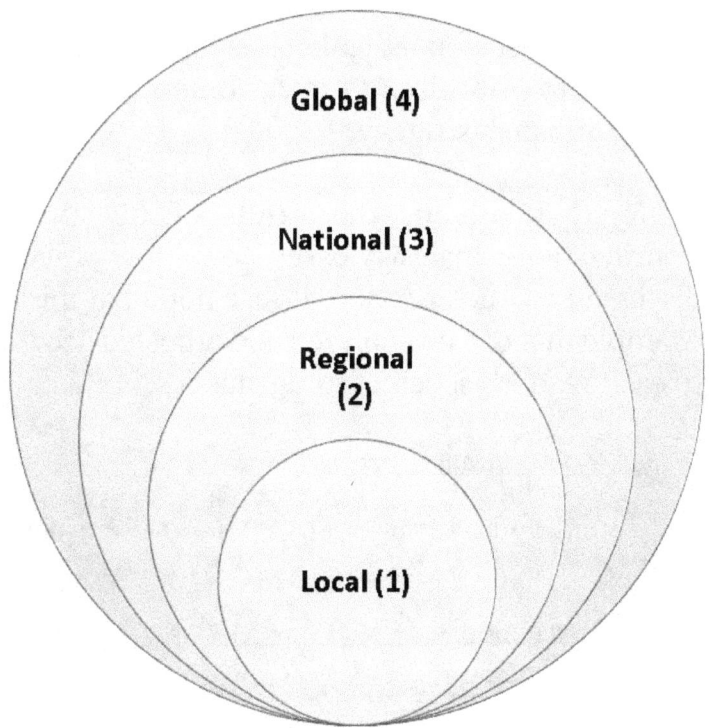

Figure 20 Analysis of coverage

Priority of prospects

Once all the variables mentioned above have been analyzed:

- o *Market share*
- o *Categorization*
- o *Territorial coverage*

Now I focus on assigning weights to each of the variables to prioritize future customers based on the sales company's strategy.

Next, I present the result of my prospect prioritization analysis based on the previously discussed characterization. Please note that this is an example that can be analyzed and adjusted according to each reader's specific circumstances:

Example of Prioritization Formula

(2*Category (1-4) + 3*Coverage (1-4) + Market Share (0-100))

Prioritization ranges

- o   High   : 50- 120
- o   Average: 30- 49
- o   Low   : 0 - 29

The following is the outcome of the revised case:

Category	Customer	Coverage	Market share	Prioritization
Innovator (3)	AA	Local (1)	5% (5)	LOW (6+3+5) =14
Leader (4)	JKO	Global (4)	35% (35)	HIGH (8+12+35) =55
Follower (2)	ABA	National (2)	20% (20)	AVERAGE (4+ 6+20) =30
Conservative (1)	GARTA	Global (4)	20% (20)	LOW (2+12 +20) *0,5=17
Innovator (3)	HUI	Regional (3)	10% (10)	AVERGAE (6+9+10) *0,5=12,5

68

Figure 21Prospect projection analysis

Note: *This prioritization is provided as an example, and the number of variables, their distribution, and the values assigned to each variable may vary for individual readers and their specific sales processes.*

Additionally, it is important to regularly review the values assigned to each prospect in conjunction with monitoring and controlling future customers. This ensures that any changes in parameters or circumstances are considered and that we are aware that these may have affected the prioritization of prospects.

Results of a prioritization example

Below, an example of what a prioritization outcome would look like for different future customers.

Where it is shown that the focus should be on contacting high-priority prospects in the first instance, followed by lower-priority prospects further down the list.

From Engineering to Sales

Prospect	Prioritization	Focus
Prospect 10	97	HIGH
Prospect 9	80	HIGH
Prospect 2	78	HIGH
Prospect 1	68	HIGH
Prospect 7	45	AVERAGE
Prospect 3	35	AVERAGE
Prospect 4	10,3	LOW
Prospect 5	9	LOW
Prospect 6	7,1	LOW
Prospect 8	5,8	LOW

Figure 2222 Prospect prioritization detail

A graphical way to represent the results is as follows:

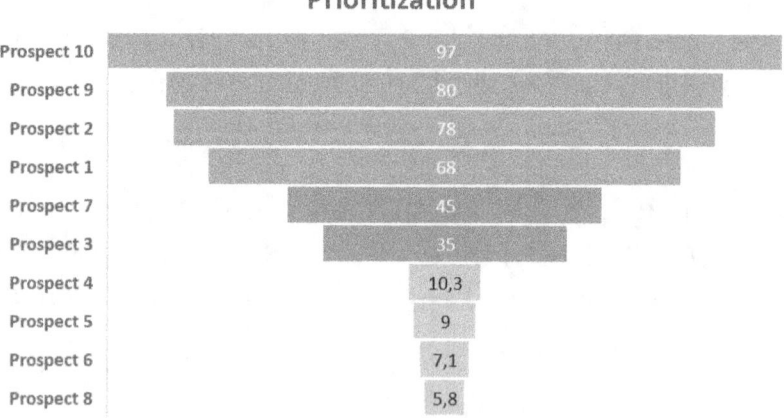

Figure 23 Prospect prioritization chart

First contacts

After completing the process of identifying and prioritizing future customers, it is crucial to contact them directly. Initially, it may be challenging to reach out to prospects whom you are not familiar with, but as you progress through the sales process, you gain more confidence in approaching new prospects. Conducting this process effectively is essential for making progress in the sales journey.

For this process you can use different communication channels, such as:

- o A phone call.
- o Text messages through messaging apps like WhatsApp, Telegram, Signal, etc.
- o email.
- o Contact through social networks such as: LinkedIn, Twitter, Facebook, etc.

A relevant issue that I learned doing this process is that each future customer has his favorite *communication channel*. The objective at this stage is to connect with the prospect and effectively communicate your message.

In today's world, younger generations tend to prefer text messaging as their primary communication channel, while previous generations still prefer phone calls and face-to-face interactions for contact. It's important to adapt to these preferences and use the appropriate communication channels to effectively engage with different target audiences.

Therefore, it is important to determine the generation to which your future customer belongs and their preferred communication channels. This understanding will help you tailor your approach and use the most effective communication methods to engage with them successfully.

What to say on that first cold call?

I remember when I made my first cold call, it took me a while to gather the courage to make the call. However, I found that preparing a script beforehand gave me the confidence and structure to guide the conversation with the new customer.

My initial script for the first cold contact was something in the line of:

1) **A courteous greeting**.
2) *An introduction of myself* with my name and company's name.
3) **The solution** that my product presented followed by its benefits.

4) **A call to action** by setting up a remote or face-to-face meeting at some time.

5) **Positive Answer:** If the answer is positive, specify the appointment's time and attach a brochure of the product or service.

6) **Negative Answer:** If the answer is no, thank him for his time and leave the doors open for a next opportunity.

7) **A pleasant farewell regardless** of the response of the potential customer.

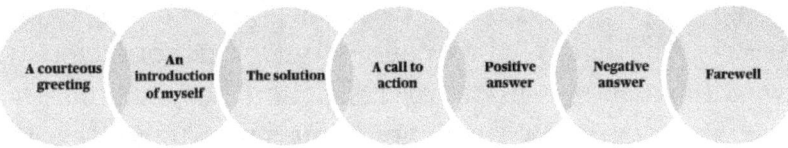

2424 Diagram for cold calls

Contacting a potential customer in a cold outreach can indeed be a new and stressful experience. It's important to be prepared for various scenarios and different responses from the person you're contacting. This includes being ready for a range of reactions and being equipped to handle a "no" response gracefully. By anticipating different outcomes and having a well-prepared approach, you can navigate these situations with confidence and professionalism. Remember that each interaction is an opportunity to learn and refine your approach, regardless of the outcome.

Indeed, negative responses are a common part of the sales process, and it's crucial to handle them with kindness, courtesy, and empathy. It's important to remember that the response is not a reflection of you or your performance personally. By understanding this, you can approach cold contacts with a mindset that is less affected by rejection.

The client who reaches out or is contacted may have a multitude of tasks and responsibilities to handle during their day. Your aim is to address their needs and provide solutions that alleviate their workload.

Another important aspect is that customers prefer to engage in conversations where they can actively contribute rather than being sold to. Therefore, the initial contact with your future customer plays a pivotal role in establishing a meaningful connection.

Here is an example of a first cold call:

Call 1: *"Good afternoon, Mr. Blandid. My name is Richard Buganvilla, and the reason of my call is to introduce our WaterFree solution. It addresses water quality issues and can provide a 30% improvement in quality and savings on additives within two days. We would be delighted to demonstrate the product and its benefits. If you could spare 30 minutes of your time, would you be available sometime this week for a discussion?"*

Future customer 1: *"I'm not interested."*

Answer to call 1: *"Dear Mr. Blandid, I appreciate your time. If you ever have any further need or questions, please feel free to reach out to me via email. Thank you very much for your time and have a great day. Goodbye!"*

You may receive many responses like these until someone on your list of prospective customers indicates interest in progressing to the next call, as the one below:

Call 2: *"Good afternoon, Mr. Blandid. My name is Richard Buganvilla, and the reason of my call is to introduce our WaterFree solution. It addresses water quality issues and can provide a 30% improvement in quality and savings on additives within two days. We would be delighted to demonstrate the product and its benefits. If you could spare 30 minutes of your time, would you be available sometime this week for a discussion?"*

Future customer 2: *"We could meet this Thursday at 3:00 p.m. in my office. I am free at that time, the address is..."*

Answer call 2: *"... Perfect, I'll be there. Please provide me with your email so I can send you a confirmation and reserve the appointment right away. I will also attach a brochure of our product, detailing its functionalities and the benefits it offers. Feel free to invite anyone you deem appropriate to the meeting. Thank you for your time, and I look forward to meeting you."*

Note: *These situations can occur through any of the communication channels previously mentioned. The important thing is to acquire new customers and make progress in the sales process, regardless of the specific communication channel used.*

The goal is to establish a connection with potential customers and effectively present the benefits of your product or service.

Stakeholder analysis

After contacting the initial set of prospective customers, it became necessary to analyze their level of interest and suitability for further progression in the sales process. This involved conducting a detailed analysis of each company on the list of potential customers:

1. The initial step is to search for and identify the relevant contacts within each company that you have reached out to and who might potentially become your future customers.

    a. For this purpose, you can use social networks (LinkedIn, Facebook, etc.), your own contacts and networks, directories, company website, industry sites, reports, etc.

2. Once the contacts within each company have been identified, the next step is to determine the various roles and interests involved in the purchasing process. This includes understanding *who* will be responsible for managing the product or service, who has the authority to authorize the purchase, and who will be using the product or service.

    a. For example, suppose you sell maintenance software. The different roles that can be identified are:

        i. *The users* Engineers, technicians, and operators of the maintenance area, who can technically validate the product.

  ii. *The managers* who are responsible for overseeing the acquisition of the product or service. This may include roles such as a purchasing analyst and a purchasing manager who are in charge of managing the entire purchasing process. In addition to these managers, it is also important to consider the involvement of the legal department, as they will review the contract or agreement between the parties involved.

  iii. *Manager of the Area* or, in some cases, the *CEO or Board of Directors*. This individual holds the decision-making authority and will ultimately determine whether to proceed with the purchase of the product and/or service.

3. Once you have identified the different contacts and roles within the company, your next step is to find a *Sponsor* who can internally champion the purchase of your product or service. The Sponsor is someone within the organization who believes in the value of your

offering and actively advocates for its adoption. They play a crucial role in influencing and persuading other stakeholders in the company about the benefits and merits of your product or service.

The key to connecting with customers.

I want to share a story to illustrate the importance of connecting with customers, during a prospecting trip. This story revolves around the initial meetings that took place, which played a crucial role in advancing the sales process.

Some time ago, I had the opportunity to go on a prospecting trip with a seasoned salesman, who we will call David, who had years of experience in consultative sales. Throughout our journey, I observed something remarkable about David's approach. In every initial meeting we had with various companies in the sector, he consistently managed to uncover new sales opportunities that ended with phone exchanges and a closing embrace.

During the trip, I was truly amazed by the process I witnessed. The presentations of the product's functionalities were often brief or even nonexistent. Instead, what stood out was the pleasant and extensive conversation about the needs and benefits of the potential customers. It was fascinating to see that the discussions went beyond the product itself and delved into more personal and social aspects of the clients.

During the trip I said to David: "... I've changed my perception about the effectiveness of the sales process. I noticed, that if our initial meetings don't create a first connection with the prospective customer, then we don't move on to the next step." He chuckled warmly in response to my comment.

The trip came to an end, and I was amazed to see that in every prospecting meeting we had, there was a closing gesture—a firm handshake or even a warm embrace. It was during these moments that we exchanged contact information, further solidifying our commitment to move forward in the sales process. What surprised me even more was that approximately 90% of the leads we met were genuinely interested in taking the next steps with us. It was a remarkable outcome, and it reinforced the value of connecting with customers on a deeper level.

To understand David's process, I asked him how he managed to capture customers' attention and drove them to move forward after the first meeting? and this was his response:

" ... Each person has unique hobbies and interests, whether it's sports, technology, family, and some are even excited to generate new business, etc. If you can determine beforehand or during the meeting about these, then you will connect with the client outside of the product or service you are trying to sell. You will be able to gain trust and empathy to advance in the process so that the real needs can be identified. We never talk about prices or any contract issue in the first meeting."

Then he continued: "the key to the whole process lies in the initial phase of the meetings. During this stage, before diving into the main agenda, it is important to introduce yourself and bring up topics that may interest the future customer. By observing their reactions and responses, you can analyze their interests and concerns. This requires a combination of empathy and experience in dealing with various types of customers."

Here is the next most important thing I learned about sales:

" Empathizing, establishing an emotional connection with the future customer, and earning their trust is key to advancing in the sales process. If you do not establish that connection and obtain their trust; you do not sell."

In the next chapter we will continue to delve into the issue of trust, since it is relevant for the preparation phase of the sale.

Previous experience in engineering to sell.

Believe it or not, my previous experience in engineering, specifically in solving complex problems, has proven to be extremely valuable in my new role. By transitioning from solving technical and engineering problems to addressing real business situations for my future customers. I can understand the core problems they face and analyze how my product or service can effectively address their needs.

Other important factors I had to develop were my soft and social skills, which included *self-management, leadership, flexibility, and empathy* to be able to put yourself in their shoes and understand their needs from their perspective.

Finally, drawing on my previous experience in the engineering field, I can quickly grasp and comprehend the technical intricacies of the product or service being offered. This enables me to thoroughly prepare for sales engagements and effectively communicate the value proposition to prospective customers.

Interpersonal skills

As I mentioned earlier, I recognized the importance of developing strong social skills in my sales role. Over time, I understood that these skills were essential for effectively connecting with unfamiliar individuals, establishing a rapport, and building trust. This, in turn, laid the foundation for customers to recognize the value and benefits of the product or service I was offering, leading to successful sales outcomes.

The social skills that need to be cultivated and fostered are:

o   assertive **listening**.

o   **Empathy** (put yourself in the place of your future customer) with the aim of generating trust.

o   Be willing to **negotiate** all objections and needs of the future customer.

o   **Collaborate** with your future customer in seeking benefits that allow them to buy.

o   **Communicate in a clear and simple way the topics**, before, during and after the sales process.

o   **Lead** the sales process, both within your organization and for your future customer.

o **Manage and resolve** all objections and negative responses until the sale is achieved.

o Build **relationships** *of trust and be transparent* about the benefits, scope of the service and limitations of your product or service.

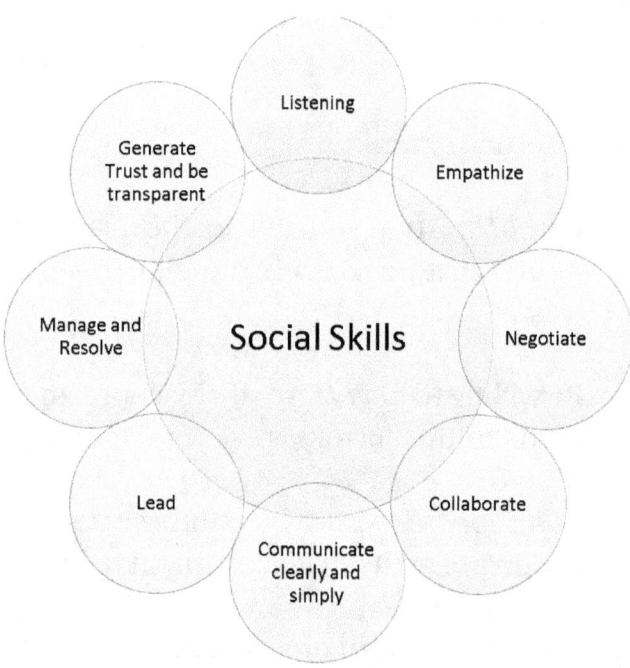

Figure 25 Social skills for sales

Using the senses over logic in selling

One important lesson I've learned through numerous iterations in the sales process is that customers don't make purchases solely based on logic. Instead, they are motivated by how well your product or service meets their needs, resonates with their emotions, and how it increases their **level of confidence** and reduces their sense of **uncertainty**.

For example, let's consider a customer who faces a recurring issue in their delivery area with the orders from their logistics operator. This problem leads to difficulties in reconciling internal and external information, resulting in inaccurate end-of-month results. The constant stress and anxiety caused by this situation create a pressing need for a solution that can provide accurate and reliable data to the company's management.

As a proposed solution, the seller suggests implementing a system that automates the daily reconciliation process, offering error detection and correction functionalities. This system enables the generation of real-time reports throughout the month, providing accurate results for management. By streamlining the process and ensuring data accuracy, it offers the customer a significant reduction in anxiety and stress levels associated with their monthly reporting tasks.

This example shows how to solve a business problem, but also includes an additional component, which is to reduce the stress level of the future customer by delivering more accurate data and reports month by month.

Finally, it is essential to remember that consultative selling relies on *building a relationship of trust* between individuals, specifically between you as the seller and your future customer. This holds true regardless of whether you are selling innovative services, products, or cutting-edge technologies.

How to build trust with your future customer?

As I said previously, a fundamental point in consultative sales is to generate trust, empathy, and credibility in the future customer. The question I asked myself was:

Why is building trust, empathy, and credibility so important for selling?

The answer was that it is imperative to understand that without the customer's trust in you and the value of your offering, they may be hesitant to share their main problems or provide crucial information about their company. This lack of trust can hinder their willingness to purchase your product or service.

Therefore, building trust with the customer is essential to progress in the sales process.

Equally important is the ability to empathize with your customer's problems and needs. By putting yourself in their shoes and understanding their unique challenges, you can gain deeper insights into their core problems. Failing to empathize with your customer may result in a disconnect and hinder progress in the sales process.

Note: *One of the key lessons I learned on the fly, is that if you can't connect, empathize, and build trust with each prospective customer; you will ultimately fail to sell. These elements are crucial in consultative sales as they lay the foundation for understanding customer needs and building meaningful relationships.*

How to create a relationship of trust with your prospect?

The question that may come to mind then is:

How do you create a relationship of trust and empathy with your future customer?

The answer is not simple since the future customer does not know you and does not trust you at the beginning of the process. However, you can generate concrete actions that will allow you to obtain their trust:

o Show your willingness to help solve the problem, regardless of whether you sell the product or service.

o The future customer must perceive you as an **expert** in the area and/or sector where you sell. It is crucial to be able to address all their doubts regarding the product and/or service, including its use, benefits, and impact on their specific needs.

o Clearly and in detail, **demonstrate the benefits** that will be obtained by solving their problems with the service or product. This empowers the future customer to effectively advocate for these benefits within their company.

o Offer a **complimentary pilot** test **at no cost**, allowing the customer to validate the benefits and address their problems and needs within a limited time frame when using the service or product.

o **Deliver on your promises**, for instance, if you promised on providing a month of free service or offering a new module with a 20% discount for the initial months, then do so.

o **Visits to your current customers,** these visits generate confidence in the future customer, since another customer is using the product or service, and can comment on their purchase, use and post-sale experience, independently of your story.

Ultimately, if the customer perceives or feels that you are not effectively addressing their needs or problems, and if the product or service doesn't meet their internal expectations for the benefits it should deliver, they will not progress further in the sales process.

How many future customers should we contact?

As previously discussed, prospecting plays a crucial role in advancing the sales process, and determining the appropriate number of customers to contact is indeed an important consideration. This analysis is influenced by two factors, which we will outline and examine in more detail in the upcoming chapters:

o Quality of prioritized prospects according to our previous profiling

o Sales Close Rate

Taking these factors into consideration, it is indeed important to establish a range of prospective customers to contact and engage with in the sales process. This range will help ensure a sufficient pool of potential clients to work with, increasing your chances of closing sales successfully.

For instance, to reach a target of 10 sales with an estimated closing rate of 10%, you would need to contact a minimum of 100 prospects. This calculation assumes that all the prospects contacted align with the quality and profile criteria that were previously defined.

Non-disclosure Agreement

During the prospecting stage, it is not uncommon for potential customers to request the signing of a non-disclosure agreement (NDA) before proceeding further in the sales process. This agreement ensures that sensitive information shared between the parties remains confidential. To be prepared for such situations, it is advisable to have a standard NDA ready to be sent to customers who require it.

Chapter 5: Preparing the Sale

By the time, I had a clear understanding of my target audience and the market, I was going to sell in, it was time to prepare the necessary elements to effectively showcase and present my product or service to potential customers. This involved creating compelling sales materials, such as brochures, presentations, demos, or samples, that accurately conveyed the features, benefits, and value proposition of what I was offering.

The key to executing this step of the sales process effectively is **early detection and understanding of the client's needs and problems**, as well as their priority in resolving them. By gaining a deep understanding of their specific challenges, you can tailor your proposal and solution to address their unique needs. This gives you greater control over the entire sales process, increasing the likelihood of a successful outcome.

Thus, a well-crafted proposal highlights the value and benefits of your solution, enabling the customer to recognize its potential impact and advantages. It aligns their needs with your offering, increasing their understanding and receptiveness to move forward in the sales process.

Do not sell functionality, solve problems.

Understanding the customer's dislike for being sold a product or service they don't need or that doesn't align with their desired benefits is crucial in sales. It is important to identify the **central problem and unique need** that the prospect is seeking to solve.

Determining the right alignment between your offering and the need of the future customer is crucial in the consultative sales process.

Always ensure that the sales process with a future customer is personalized and tailored specifically to them. Make them feel valued as an individual client, so they do not feel this is just another transaction for your company. This might include customizing the product and/or service you are offering to meet their unique needs and preferences.

The objective at this stage is to prepare a presentation or pilot that focuses on helping the future customer solve their problem or central need. It's important to avoid giving the impression that the sole intention is to sell the product or service. Instead, the focus should be on providing value and addressing their specific challenges.

Understanding the needs.

As previously stated, understanding the needs and the central problem are essential elements at this stage to continue advancing in the process. To gain understanding of these, it is imperative to establish a **bond of trust** and empathy with your future customer. This connection will enable you to analyze their needs and identify the **central problem** they are seeking to solve. By understanding their challenges, you can effectively demonstrate how your product or service can help address the problem and deliver the associated benefits.

The central problem can often be obscured by other needs and secondary issues on the customer's problems list.

One of the key drivers of success in the sales process is accurately understanding the central problem and presenting customized solutions and benefits that address it. This approach empowers the future customer to make an informed decision and progress further in the sales process.

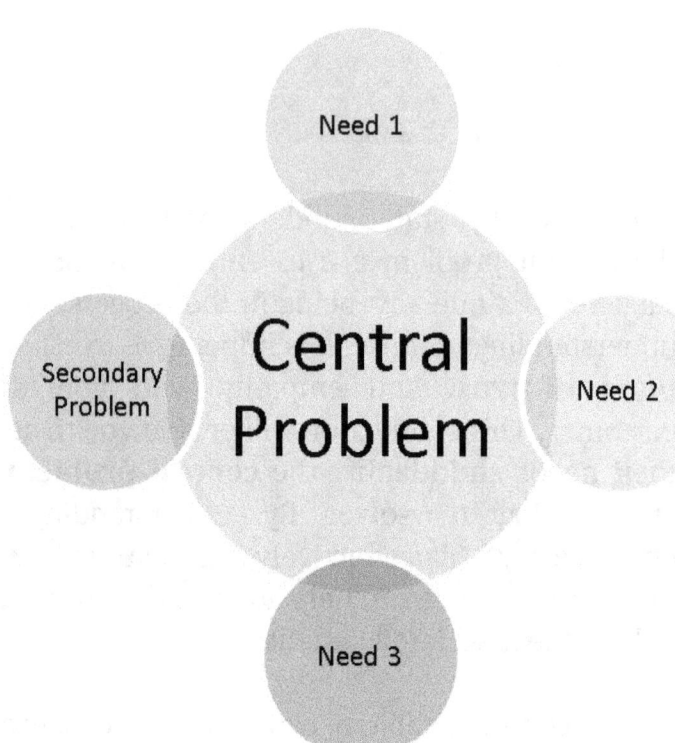

Figure 26 Central problem

What to ask to find out what their real needs are?

Initially, due to my lack of experience, I found myself asking this question as I realized I was having too many meetings without obtaining the necessary information I needed. Through self-reflection, I discovered the importance of asking targeted questions and actively listening during interactions with prospective customers. These techniques help to uncover their genuine needs and central problem, which serve as the focal point for advancing in the sales process.

Below are some of the questions I began asking future customers during meetings, interviews, and presentations. These questions are divided into two categories: general questions to capture the customer's attention and detailed questions to understand their needs more in depth.

General Questions

- What are your main motivations for discussing our product and/or service currently?

- What specific goals or insights are you hoping to achieve or gain by reviewing our product or service today?

- Where and how do you see your company in the future after solving your problems?

- To achieve the objective of this meeting, which specific topics would you like to address?

These initial open-ended questions are designed to gather insights about their current situation, needs, problems, and desired outcomes. By understanding their responses, we can gain a broad vision and a comprehensive understanding of how we can assist them.

Afterwards, by utilizing the following detailed questions below, we can further explore their problems and needs, by narrowing down the specific scope of the issue. This will enable us to analyze potential solutions that may be viable in addressing their unique challenges.

Detailed Questions

- Could you please provide a description of the specific situation that gives rise to the problem or need you are seeking to address?

- For how long has the situation that gives rise to the problem or need you are seeking to address been ongoing?

- From their perspective you can separate or aggregate the situation into one or more than one problem or need.

- In your opinion, which of the described problems do you consider to be the most important to address and solve at this time?

- Which departments or areas of the company are affected by the situation described above?

- What is the periodicity of occurrence of the situation?

- If the situation described above is not resolved, what impact and consequences do you anticipate it will have on your business?

- What is the level of urgency or priority given to resolve this situation?

- What direct impact does this problem or situation generate in your daily work?

- Would you have the authority to make the decision to address and solve the problem directly, or would you require someone else's approval or go through a tender process?

Note: *When asking these questions, it is important to take thorough notes of each answer and refrain from interrupting your future customer while they are providing their response.*

The following is an outline of possible topics to identify in your meetings with the potential customer:

- Problems
- Needs
- Interests

o Decision makers
o Sponsor
o Central problem
o Priority needs.
o Roles in the organization

This summary scheme can be customized for each meeting with the future customer, serving as a foundation for preparing a proposal that aligns closely with their needs and requirements.

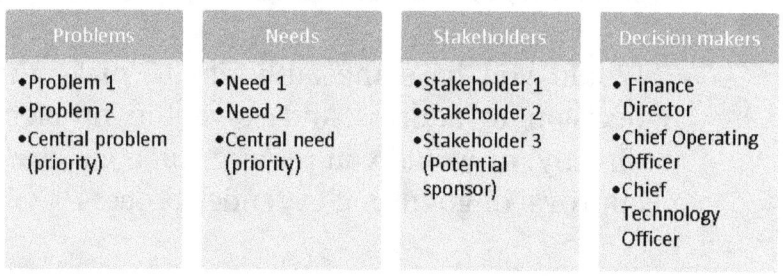

Problems	Needs	Stakeholders	Decision makers
•Problem 1 •Problem 2 •Central problem (priority)	•Need 1 •Need 2 •Central need (priority)	•Stakeholder 1 •Stakeholder 2 •Stakeholder 3 (Potential sponsor)	• Finance Director •Chief Operating Officer •Chief Technology Officer

Figure 27 Understanding the potential customer.

What to do when a customer cannot define its needs?

Sometimes, future customers may be unaware of a specific problem but can perceive it based on the end output or results they achieve. For instance, a prospect may recognize a production problem when they fail to meet the goals set by their company's shareholders. However, they may not have identified the central or root cause of the issue and only perceive the symptoms through the results.

In such scenario, it is important for you to take an active role as an **expert consultant in the industry** you are selling to. Your objective is to help the customer find and diagnose the central problem they are facing. By doing so, you can demonstrate that their problem can be effectively addressed with your product and/or service. Your role is to convince the customer that by solving the central problem, they can achieve the desired benefits and meet their goals within a specified timeframe.

Never fix *the price* at the beginning

This topic is relevant because some future customers may inquire about the price of the product or service before discussing their problems or specifying what they are seeking to solve. This situation can create difficulties in the consultative sales process since without identifying the need or central problem, there is a lack of clarity regarding the appropriate solution, the scope of the service, and the specific product that should be offered to the future customer.

So, when a future customer asks about the price at the beginning of the sales process, it is better to be transparent and explain that the price will depend on their specific problems and needs, as it will determine the appropriate product or service associated with the solution they require.

If the future customer insists on getting a price range while you are still in the process of understanding their needs and problems, you can provide a rough estimate but emphasize that it may vary based on the final solution.

How to understand the customer's needs?

As mentioned earlier, it is crucial to have a detailed understanding of the client's **needs and problems**, as well as the potential impact on their business when these issues are resolved.

Once you have identified and gathered a list of needs from the client, the next step is to prioritize them based on the client's perceived importance to their business. This prioritization helps you understand which needs should be addressed first and which ones are of lesser significance. With this prioritized list, you can then prepare a value proposition that aligns your product or service with the solution that effectively addresses these needs, starting from the highest-priority ones down to the lower-priority ones. This approach ensures that your proposal focuses on providing the maximum benefits and value to the client's business.

For this prioritization process, the following list of needs and benefits can be generated:

Need	Functionality	Benefit	Coverage	Priority
Need 1	Functionality A and B	Sales increase	60%	High
Need 2	Functionality C and D	Low rejection rate	90%	Medium
Need 4	Functionality D	Productivity Increase	100%	Medium
Need 3	Functionality G	Decrease in rework	80%	Low

Figure 28 Needs analysis.

Depending on this prioritization, the needs can be ordered as follows:

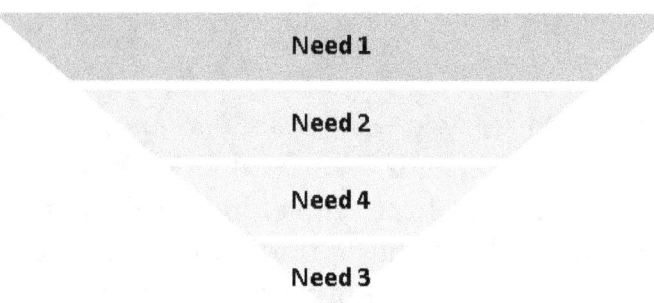

Figure 29 Standardization of priorities

This approach allows you to address the needs of higher priority first in your proposal (as they will provide the most significant benefits to the future customer) moving downwards to the remaining ones.

Define the future customer's route.

During all interactions with the future customer, it is essential to prioritize transparency and clarity when explaining the sales process. Providing a clear roadmap helps them understand the next steps and encourages their engagement in the buying process. Here are some examples of defined routes for different potential customers:

- o Initial contact- Demonstration of the product or service - proposal - Negotiations and Close.

- o Initial contact - Demonstration of the product or service - Pilot - Visit to current customers (on demand) - Proposal - Negotiations and Closure.

- o Initial contact - Demonstration 1 - proposal - Negotiation1 - Demonstration 2 - proposal 2- Negotiation 2 and Close

- o Other variants of the previous ones.

Each of these options, as well as others that may arise, will vary depending on the type of client, their motivations, and priorities. It is important to align the steps of the sales process with the defined guidelines in your company. Additionally, it is highly recommended to keep the process *simple and efficient to ensure success in the sale*. An **agile process** that provides a positive shopping experience for the future customer is key.

Trust and empathy as the central point in the sale of services

As I gained more experience in selling services, I realized that the sales process for this becomes more complex as compared to selling products. Selling intangible services requires establishing trust and empathy with clients. It is essential to demonstrate a deep knowledge and expertise in the sector you are selling to build credibility. By positioning yourself as an expert consultant, you can instill confidence in clients and effectively address their needs and concerns.

In addition to establishing trust and empathy, it is of utmost importance to showcase your consultative knowledge in the field. Excellent communication skills are essential in clearly conveying the tangible and intangible benefits of your service. To strengthen your message, you can provide examples of success stories and facilitate interviews with satisfied customers who have experienced the value of your service firsthand.

Stakeholder map

One helpful tool that aided me in understanding the stakeholders is the *Stakeholder map*. This visual representation allows for a clear visualization of the various roles within the client organization and their respective interests. By engaging in multiple interactions and meetings with different stakeholders, you can develop a comprehensive understanding of each individual's perspective and priorities. Over time, this process enables you to gain valuable insights into the dynamics and needs of the client organization as a whole.

The objective of creating a Stakeholder Map is to provide a clear overview of where to focus efforts when engaging with different stakeholders in the sales process. This map serves as a guide and can be adjusted as the sales process progresses and new insights are gained through interactions with various stakeholders.

This map considers four types of stakeholders that determine the continuation in the purchase process:

o **Motivated to buy.**

> In this area, you will find stakeholders who are receptive and convinced that your solution, products, and/or services can effectively address their problems and deliver the desired benefits. Additionally, it is possible to find candidates for sponsors of our products and / or services.

o **Not convinced to buy**

> In this area, you will find stakeholders who have expressed objections or concerns regarding various aspects such as the solution, functionalities, price, benefits, conditions, and more. These stakeholders are critical to the

sales process as addressing their objections is key to moving forward.

o **Indifferent to the purchase process**

This group of uninterested parties has no position on the matter since they have no direct relationship with the purchase. This group is not the initial focus of your sales process.

o **Against buying**

This group of interested parties is the one that blocks the sales process. The objective is to identify the underlying reasons for their hesitations or objections, which can stem from technical concerns, financial constraints, business priorities, time constraints, or potential direct or indirect impacts on their roles or responsibilities.

An example of a stakeholder map below.

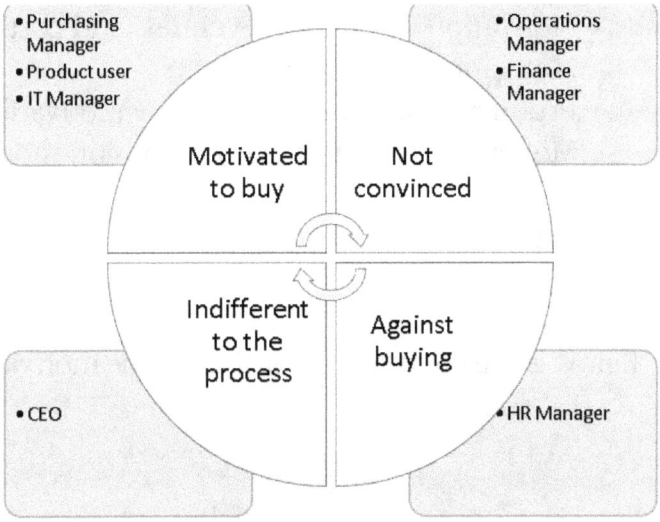

Figure 30 Stakeholder map

Stakeholder motivations

Another perspective that complements the stakeholder map and helps to understand them in depth is to analyze the motivations of each role within the organization.

This analysis allows you to discover their specific goals and objectives related to the purchase of the product and/or service.

Some common motivations you may come across include:

o Motivation in processes

- o Motivation in results, revenues, and costs.
- o Motivation in people.
- o Product or service functionality motivation.
- o Motivation on monetary and non-monetary benefits.
- o Other.

Below is the commented outline of the motivations.

Figure 31 Motivations

By understanding the various visions and motivations within the organization, you can effectively address the objections raised by each stakeholder during the sales process. For instance:

- o **Processes**: Understand how the product or service improves the process where the problem exists.

- o **People**: Measure the positive effects on people by using the product or service.

- o **Functionalities**: Explode the key functionalities that can serve future users.

- o **Benefits**: Detail the benefits, both monetary and non-monetary, that would be obtained with the use of the product or service.

- o **Revenues and Costs**: Detail the costs and the revenues with the use of the service or product over time.

If you manage to understand each of these objections, you can clarify and propose solutions that will allow you to unlock the sales process.

Identify your audience.

One of the relevant topics to find out before participating in any meeting, is identifying the types of profiles that will be present in the meeting. This allows for tailored focus, content, and style to effectively engage participants. These audiences can be categorized in various types such as:

o   Technical audience

o   Technical, commercial, etc.

o   Both

Meetings should stem from this criterion as this enables you to customize the focus, topics, and questions to effectively address the specific needs and interests of each profile. This not only maximizes engagement but also leads to more productive outcomes and successful meetings overall.

Technical audience

The technical audience will be focused on knowing the functionality and details of how to solve the problems and needs with the product or service.

Non-Technical audience and Decision Makers

The **Non-Technical audience**, being focused on the practical aspects, will indeed be interested in understanding the immediate and future benefits of using the product or service. They will specifically seek insights into how it can impact the company's revenues, costs, and provide solutions to their current financial needs and problems.

It is important to highlight the tangible financial value and demonstrate how the product or service aligns with their technical requirements, ensuring that they perceive it as a valuable investment.

Preparation of the presentation

Effective communication with future customers is key, and a well-prepared presentation can greatly contribute to achieving this goal.

A few well-structured questions that will allow **you to** understand and help achieve the objective you are looking for are:

What:
- o What are you looking to obtain from the presentation of the product and / or service?

  In general, when answering this question, it is important to confirm the **main objective**

111

you want to convey in the product or service presentation and **avoid covering more than two central topics**. The focus of the meeting should be on specific objectives such as showing the benefits of the product or service, discovering the core problem faced by the audience, advancing in the closing of the sales process, showcasing product functionality along with its benefits, or presenting success stories and demonstrations. By keeping the presentation focused on these key areas, you can effectively engage the audience and drive the meeting towards achieving the desired outcomes.

Who:

o   Who will be participating in the meeting?

The answer must be based on the profile of each participant (technical, commercial, financial, etc.). and their role in the organization (user, boss, manager, decision maker, etc.). Based on this premise, the content of your presentation will change as we previously analyzed.

Why:

o Why is it important to buy the product or service from the point of view of the future customer?

This question is relevant since it connects the **main need and problem with the benefits of the product and/or service**. The benefits must support the reason for the purchase, so your presentation must reinforce it.

Prepare the story script.

When preparing any presentation, I have found it valuable to incorporate a well-crafted story as a central element. A compelling story helps establish a connection with the audience and build trust. Creating a script for the story, including relevant topics to discuss in initial meetings, presentations, and product demonstrations, becomes crucial in guiding the entire process. It allows for a cohesive narrative that effectively communicates the value proposition and resonates with the audience, capturing their attention and generating meaningful engagement.

This script should include, for example, some key topics such as:

- o **Main problems and needs** that the product or service solves.

    - Help with unfulfilled orders.
    - Automatic monthly balance closing.
    - Automating customer analysis and typification.
    - Etc.

- o **Benefits**

    - Reduction of overtime by 5% to 20% in a one-month period.
    - Improvement in waiting times by 7% to 10% over the course of a quarter.
    - Sales increase in a range of 6% to 25% per year.
    - Production efficiency increase of 5% each semester.
    - Etc.

- o **Key features**

    - Graph of hours worked vs unproductive hours generated in real time.
    - Intelligent mailing to customers with tickets included.

- Automatic information classification algorithm to improve production.
- Etc.

Story telling

Telling stories for me was a challenge, and in general this is not an innate ability to many of us, but in sales it is very relevant when it comes to selling.

To delve into the importance of storytelling in sales, it is essential to address some of the key aspects, for example:

o Convincing your future customer that your product and/or service meets their *needs and solves their problems at a reasonable value, without having previously developed or implemented anything.*

o Reassuring that it will generate the **benefits** you point out in a certain time.

o Showcasing your product and/or service with one or more elements that **differentiate** it from the competition.

o Finally, **persuading** and **negotiating the conditions** so that they can acquire or lease your product and/or service in a limited time.

To demonstrate each of these elements to your future customer. It is necessary to frame these elements in a **story and narrative** that covers them, for example:

o *Detail how* the *product was created* to meet the identified needs. Provide a detailed account of how the product came to be, its evolution over time, and its successful launch in the market.

o *Examples of success stories with customers* who had the same or similar needs and what benefits they achieved with the use of the product or system.

o An important element to incorporate in your storytelling is highlighting the **unique aspects** that differentiate your product or service from the competition. To achieve this, you can present real case studies and showcase how your offering has made a positive impact on customers.

o **Empathize** with **your future customer** by sharing a story that resonates with their own problems and needs. By presenting a relatable narrative that reflects their challenges and aspirations, you can create a strong emotional connection. This allows the customer to see themselves in the story and perceive your product or service as a solution that can address their specific pain points.

o Lastly, it is essential for the story to have a **clear call to action** that prompts the future customer to take the next step in the sales process.

When sharing information about your product or service, it is indeed beneficial to present it in the form of a story using **simple and customer-friendly language**. By avoiding complex technical jargon or industry-specific terms, you ensure that your audience can easily understand and relate to the concepts being discussed.

Based on my experience, I have found that building a story in the sales process requires at least three key elements:

o A success story.
o A visual element that explains the problems and needs we are solving and how this is done.
o A narrative that begins with a problem, an anecdote, if possible, that includes the

solution to the problem, and the results-benefits obtained at the end of the story.

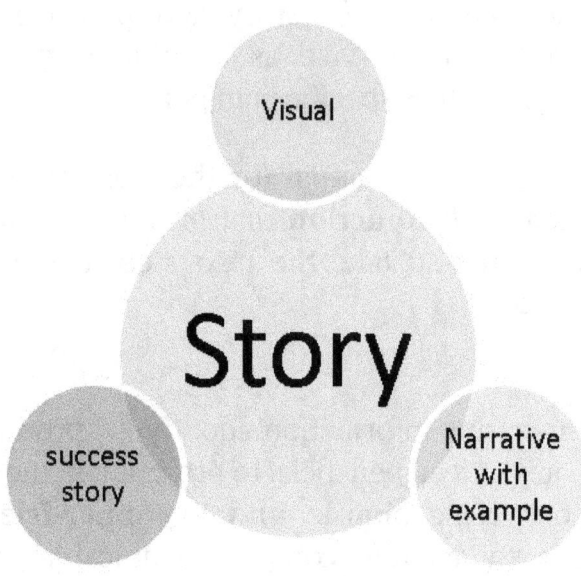

Figure 32 Building a story.

During your narratives with the client, it is essential to identify and address a need or problem that resonates with them, keeping them engaged and focused on the potential solutions offered by your product and/or service.

The story must create **authentic and transparent communication** that resonates with the future customer, establishing a strong impact. Successful sales rely on real and compelling stories to build trust and empathy, forming strong relationships with future customers.

Present the benefits.

An important lesson I learned over time is that when presenting the product and/or service, it is key to show the benefits that will be obtained, in real situations, in numerical terms and with defined deadlines, for example:

- o **Sales increase**
  - o 5% increase in sales in a period of one semester.

- o **Savings in staffing hours**
  - o Savings of three hundred staffing hours in the operations area in one month.

- o **Equipment optimization**
  - o Improve equipment usage to reduce downtime by 20% per month.

- o **Increased production**
  - o Improvement in the production process by increasing efficiency by 5% in a quarter.

- **Waste reduction**
  - Waste reduction in the production process, with a saving of 10% compared to the total inputs occupied in a semester.

Through these examples it is possible to show the benefits obtained by your customers in a certain time and with real numerical data. These serve as a basis to increase confidence in the product and/or service.

Effective presentations

Another fundamental point I learned early is that it is important to make a strong impression in the first 5 minutes of your sales presentation.

By addressing the specific needs and interests of your audience, you can capture their attention and create a connection. Avoid delivering a generic presentation that fails to resonate with individual customers. Instead, focus on personalization and tailor your message to their unique requirements.

If someone in your audience is distracted by their mobile device or computer during your presentation, it is a sign that you haven't fully engaged them or connected with them, and you have more or less lost them.

Engaging your audience from the beginning is crucial for building rapport and increasing the likelihood of a successful outcome.

Some ideas for making an **effective** presentation are:

o Use a *simple, straightforward language* to explain your presentation.

o *Use large letters* so that the entire audience can see them from anywhere in the auditorium or room.

o *Tone and body language* are key to the good reception of the presentation message. Increase the tone to highlight a key point and stop for a moment before commenting on the relevant topic to fix the message in the audience.

o Start your presentation by providing a general overview of the topic, and then gradually transition into more specific details. Use **practical examples** and keep the language simple and easily understandable for your audience. **This approach helps to ensure that** everyone can follow along and grasp the concepts you're presenting.

o Ensure that each slide of your presentation focuses on conveying a single idea or message. Stick to a maximum of two to three main ideas per presentation, allowing each concept to be effectively communicated and understood by your audience.

o Make your presentations and **demonstrations interactive** by actively engaging with the audience. Encourage participation by asking questions related to the topics you're discussing and invite the audience to share any doubts or questions they may have. This not only keeps the audience involved but also allows you to address any concerns or clarify any misunderstandings in real time.

o *Paraphrase their questions* and speak their language to build connection with auditors.

o *Do not mix text in small paragraphs with graphics* or outlines, as your audience may focus on trying to read rather than listening and visualizing. Use concise and visually appealing slides that support your main points.

o Add simple outlines and explanations with *an idea per schema.*

o Support the main message or idea of the presentation with *stories of other clients or users* (with recommendations previously reviewed).

In the first meeting, you must generate interest in the benefits of the product or services you provide. If the client can relate any of these outlined points to their specific needs and central problem, they are more likely to continue in the sales process.

A suggested structure for an initial first presentation can last between 15 to 20 minutes maximum, the rest of the time you can use it to ask about needs and problems.

Here is a suggested standard scheme for the presentation:

1. Company introduction (2 min)
2. Product or service presentation (2 min)
3. Benefits of the product or service (5 min)
4. Functionality to support benefits (5 min)
5. Success stories (2 min)
6. Next steps (1 min)

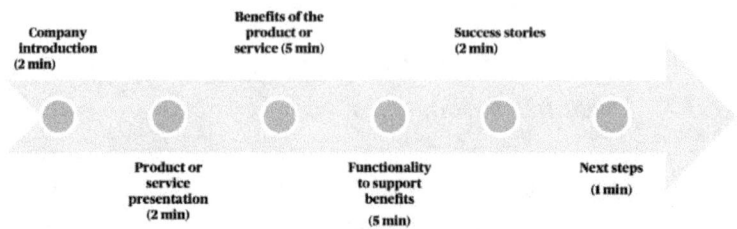

Figure 33 Order of an initial presentation

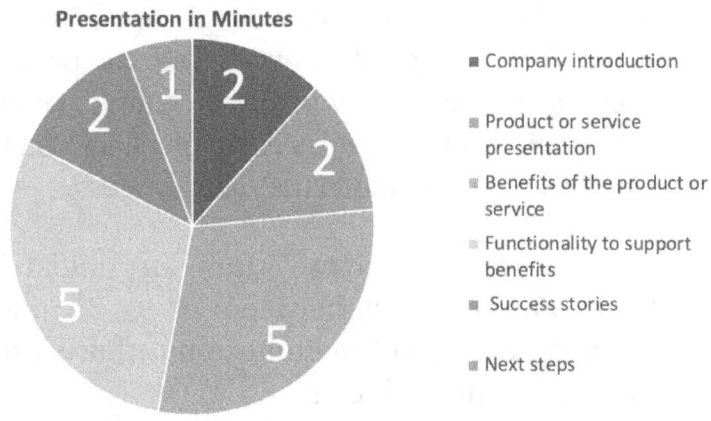

Figure 34 Temporary outline of an initial presentation

Note: *If you receive questions, in any of the sections of the presentation, you are on the right track, since there is an interest in understanding your proposal.*

One thing I learned over the course of many meetings with clients during all **these sales** processes **is that** in terms of content your presentation must be *original and focused on solving the problem or need.* The future customer must feel that your product or service is adding value to their business.

Demonstrations

The first point to prepare the demonstration is to determine the type of audience as we saw previously, if the audience is technical, economic, **or** a mixture of both, since this will condition the type of demonstration of the product or service.

Given the type **of audience,** prepare your demo beforehand, validate the accesses, connections (if remote), cases and examples to show **to** the audience. In order to choose the cases **to** show during **the** demonstration, you will have to use the information you got in your initial contact as a basis **and** some other case that generates high impact and relevant benefits for the future customer.

In every demonstration, the first 5 minutes are key to captivate the audience. By generating curiosity and the need to see the demonstration, you gain an important window of time for the customer to follow your story.

One of the biggest mistakes I made when I started on this topic of performing a demo was:

o Show one hour all the functionality of the product you wanted to sell and without any benefit.

o Within 10 minutes the customer was bored, and we did not move on to the next stage of the sales process.

o In the end I could not connect with their needs and problems.

If the proposed solution plus the benefit is connected to the need and the main problem, the customer will surely move forward in the process.

Remember that in general, a client may not utilize 100% of the functionality of your product or service. On average, they may use as little as 40%, similar to when people purchase insurance or a gym subscription. At this stage, the important thing is to determine which functionalities address their specific needs and problems effectively.

A suggested structure for a first demonstration is as follows:

1. What is the product or service of the Demo? (2 min)
2. Detail the real case to review (2 min)

3. Benefit Example   (5 min)
4. Functionality that supports the benefit   (5 min)
5. Next steps to move forward   (1 min)

What is the product or service of the Demo? (2 min)

Benefit Example (5 min)

Next steps to move forward (1 min)

Detail the real case to review (2 min)

Functionality that supports the benefit (5 min)

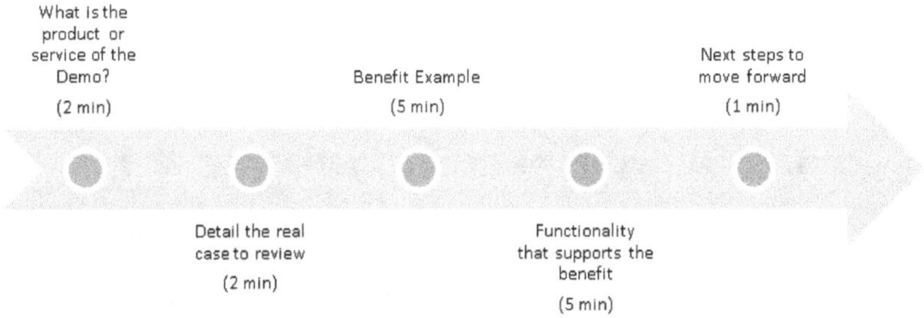

Figure 35 Outline of a demo

If you have already managed to determine the problem or central need of the future customer, you should focus the demonstration on these needs to advance in the sales process.

One thing I learned after doing quite a few demonstrations is this:

" ... *The Demonstrations should show more benefits and less functionalities. We only show the key functionalities* that *support* the *benefits of the product* and/or *service that the customer could use, and we explained them in a language they use daily.* "

Meetings and demonstrations

127

When the coronavirus pandemic hit, conducting remote meetings and demonstrations with customers became essential. It was necessary to address specific issues unique to remote interactions compared to in-person meetings. Building a strong connection with your future customers became more challenging in the virtual setting.

Some of the important topics to review before starting a meeting or a demonstration are:

1. Check your internet **connection** (Ensure the quality of your internet connection and have alternative options readily available in case of connectivity issues, such as using a mobile network or other backup connections.)

2. Test the connection and quality of your microphone and video camera.

3. Make sure the tool or software you will use for the presentation is working correctly.

4. Secure the correct position of the camera to ensure a professional and visually appealing presentation angle.

5. Choose a neutral background for your computer to avoid distractions during the presentation.

It is indeed important to start remote meetings by turning on your camera and encouraging the future customer to do the same. This visual interaction helps establish a personal connection and build trust. By seeing each other's facial expressions and body language, you can gauge the level of engagement and quickly assess whether you are effectively connecting with the customer.

Use the mouse to navigate and highlight specific topics to guide the audience's attention and ensure they stay focused.

When someone asks you a question during a meeting or presentation, it's important to *practice active listening and give them your full attention*. Avoid interrupting them, even if you already know the answer. Let the person finish their question and take a moment to process it before responding.

When you do respond, do so with **enthusiasm, empathy, and energy**. Show genuine interest in their question and provide a thoughtful and well-articulated response.

Engage in a dialogue with the person, asking follow-up questions, if necessary, to ensure you fully understand their concerns or needs. By demonstrating your attentiveness and enthusiasm, you can foster a positive and engaging atmosphere that promotes effective communication and builds trust with your audience.

Meetings, presentations, demonstrations, and pilots are good instances to identify the sponsor and decision makers to move forward in the sales process.

Searching for the sponsor

A key issue to advance in the sales process with your future customer is to be able to count on a *sponsor* within the company in which you want to sell.

The role of the *sponsor* will be responsible for promoting the existing needs and future benefits of your product or service within the company. Once the customer agrees to move forward with the purchase, they can assist you in convincing those who are still hesitant or disagree to make the same decision for your product or service.

Some questions you are probably thinking:

1. Who can be the sponsor for your product or service within the company?

   To answer this answer, you should start by reviewing some candidates, such as:

o Who was the first person you contacted or contacted to learn about the product or service?

o Who will be your future user of the product or service?

o Who will or could drive the purchase decision within the company?

o Which of all the meeting attendees felt more convinced to move forward with the purchase?

Note: *As an important note it is necessary to consider that a sponsor who has the decision-making power for the purchase can accelerate your sales process exponentially, since you will not need to climb in the command structure to buy your product or service.*

2. Where and when do I find my *Sponsor?*

To answer this question, we can mention that the Sponsor can appear at any stage of the sales process, in a presentation, demonstration, initial meeting, pilot, proposal review, etc., but will only manifest as your sponsor when they/he/she has confidence in you, your product, and/or service and understands that the benefits of your product can address their needs and problems effectively.

There may be different types of sponsors, depending on the internal decision-making power they possess. They can significantly influence and promote the purchase of the product or service within their organization.

The types of sponsors that you can identify at the time of selling will be given depending on the type and size of the company:

- o Owner or partner of the company
- o Chairman of the Board
- o Vice-president
- o CEO
- o Chief Financial Officer
- o IT Director
- o User Area Director
- o Head or direct user of the product or service
- o Current supplier of the company
- o External consultant to the company who helps in the purchase process.

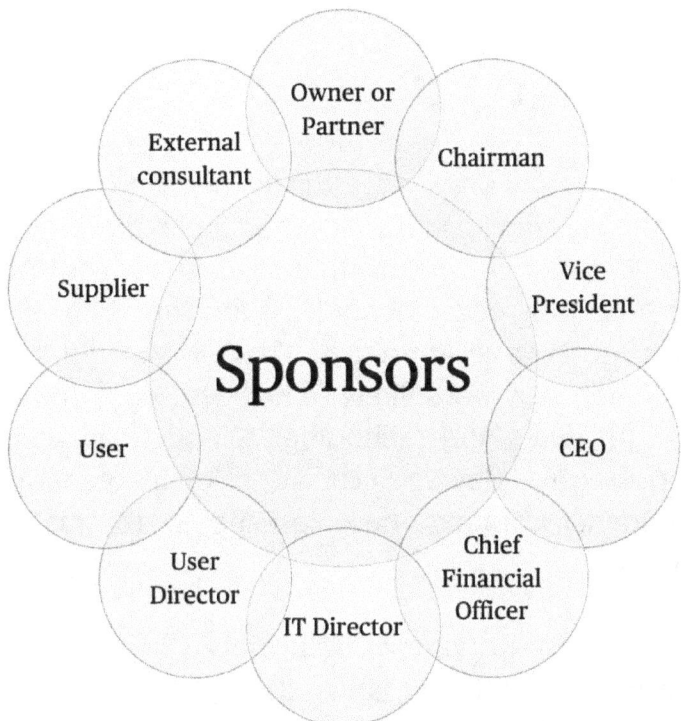

Figure 36 Potential sponsors

This list is an example of possible sponsors you can find, but not limited in terms of profiles or roles.

On the other hand, it is not an obligation to have a sponsor during the sales process, but it can be essential to streamline the process and improve your sales conversion rate.

Success stories

As discussed previously during the market analysis, if your product is new to the target market, you should target companies that are actively seeking to adopt cutting-edge technology and are known for their **innovative** approach. These forward-thinking customers are more likely to take risks and embrace new products and technologies, and their success stories can play a crucial role in generating confidence among new prospects to make a purchase.

These types of *innovative prospects* are those who will be willing to try and take the risk with your product and/or services to be first to market. These first customers will be your case study to show it to other companies that are more averse to risk and thereby advance in the process of selling to the rest of the market.

By showcasing the solutions and benefits experienced by *innovative customers*, you can effectively reach conservative companies and customers. They seek to analyze various success stories and find those that closely resemble their needs and problems. This process helps them reduce uncertainty and risk aversion, aligning with their pre-purchase vision for a successful outcome.

visits to current customers who have successfully implemented your proposed solutions are an incredibly effective and direct way to showcase success stories. These visits allow potential future customers to see firsthand how your product or service has solved real-world problems and delivered tangible benefits.

Pilots

In a consultative sale it will always be necessary to *pilot.* Piloting refers to conducting demonstrations or tests using real customer data to showcase how the product or service works in a real-world environment. It allows the future customer to experience the value and benefits of the offering firsthand.

Based on my experience, I can confidently say that it is challenging to make a sale without the future customer expressing a desire to test the benefits of the product through a pilot or test. Customers often want to validate the functionalities and capabilities of the product in their own environment before making a commitment.

The excuse I always get from every company at some point for wanting a pilot is in this mention:

"We do not consider our company as a special case in the sector, nor do we work the same as the rest of the market. therefore, we propose conducting a test to find out if the product and/or service can be adapted to our reality."

In general, prospective customers prefer to test the product within their own company, involving their teams and assessing its fit with their specific requirements, before committing to further stages of the sales process.

Pilot Plan

The plan to carry out the pilot must include a series of phases or stages to ensure its successful execution within a reasonable timeframe. Each stage of the pilot freezes the process temporarily as the focus shifts to evaluating the results and benefits of the product and/or service. The aim is to minimize the duration of each stage to expedite the overall pilot process.

- o **Step 0**: Define the plan and criteria for acceptance of the results of the pilot (quantifiable benefits for the future customer) For example:

- o Reduce waiting times by 5% compared to the current ones in a calendar month.

- o Increase production by 7% for the use of the product or service during the 2-week pilot period.

o **Step 1**: Collection of customer input data.

o **Step 2**: Configure the product or service with the data of the future customer.

o **Step 3**: Generate initial results using the product or service.

o **Step 4**: Iterate on observations and adjustments using feedback from the future customer to generate new results that are validated by the future customer.

o **Step 5**: Show the benefits of using the results product or service.

o **Step 6:** Close the pilot and take action to continue with the sales process.

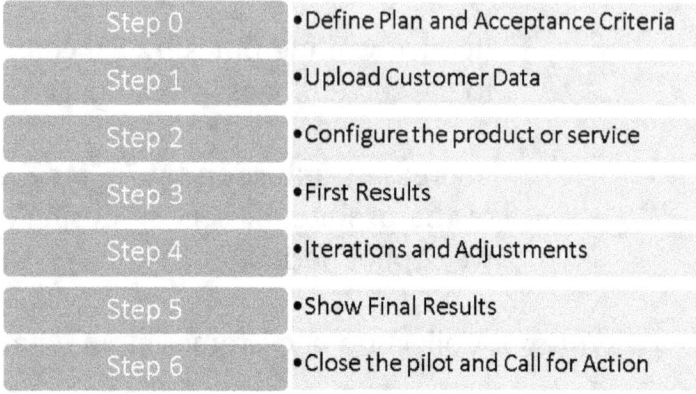

Figure 37 Schematic of a pilot

The duration of each stage and the overall plan for the pilot will vary depending on the nature of the product or service. This timeframe can range from a few days to several months. However, it is important to emphasize that shorter durations tend to generate higher expectations and increase the likelihood of moving forward. By providing an agile and efficient pilot experience, the customer gains confidence in the product or service, paving the way for further progress in the sales process.

Chapter 6: Generating a Proposal

The primary goal of presenting a proposal is to showcase the value of the service or product you are offering and clearly outline the distinctive elements of your solution that set you apart from competitors.

Marketing strategies to support your value proposal.

Marketing plays a fundamental role in crafting a compelling value proposition by associating your product and/or service with distinctive concepts that differentiate you from your competitors. The objective is to establish a robust brand positioning that drives progress in the sales process and ensures that your target market is aware of and appreciates your value proposition.

Marketing is essential for creating awareness of your product and/or service in the target market and positioning it as a brand that embodies the desired attributes and value that the selling company aims to associate with.

Note: We will not delve into the subject of marketing in this book, as there is a significant amount of literature available that addresses this topic in detail if you want to deepen your knowledge.

Value proposal for different objectives.

When presenting a value proposal to a prospect, it is crucial to provide a comprehensive outline of the value it offers in fulfilling their objectives. This entails incorporating both a technical and economic proposal that effectively addresses their primary problem and outlines the benefits they can achieve through the proposed solution.

One of the first questions you should ask before preparing the value proposition is:

Why would the future customer want to buy the product or service?

The specific interests and concepts included in a value proposal can vary based on each individual customer's needs and preferences, for example:

- o Interest in **solving the problem.**
- o Increase **safety.**
- o **Uncertainty**.
- o Getting **"status"**.

- o Follow a **trend** of a product or service.
- o Comfort.
- o **Free up time** by solving the problem or need.
- o A feeling of **pleasure**.
- o **Innovation** and new technologies.
- o Price.
- o Benefits.
- o Support for the product or service locally.

Understanding the main reasons why your prospective customer makes a purchase is essential for a successful value proposal. By identifying their motivations, you can align your product or service with those specific reasons to create a compelling association.

Figure 38 Reasons for purchase

To illustrate this point, let me share an experience from one of my sales processes where a prospect ultimately chose not to purchase my product. This example will shed light on the reasons behind their decision and help us gain a deeper understanding of their mindset.

I asked the prospect after they had signed with the competition:

Why did you make the decision of not buying our product?

And the client replied:

"The product I selected is trendy and incorporates cutting-edge technologies, enabling my company to establish itself as an innovative player in the market. Both options offered comparable prices, benefits, and functionalities, effectively addressing the core problem within my company."

This answer prompted me to realize that customers don't always make purchasing decisions based solely on the product's ability to solve their problem. There are other variables at play that go beyond pure logic and rationality.

in the sales process, it is crucial to identify the **emotional or non-logical reasons** behind a customer's purchasing decision. As we have discussed, it is not only about solving a problem and providing benefits but also about associating your product or service with **non-monetary advantages**. Just like the previous example of the fashionable product that helps create a status or image, understanding and addressing these non-monetary benefits can greatly influence the customer's perception and decision-making process.

Ultimately, it is crucial to articulate the benefits in a clear and compelling manner to convince prospective customers that your product or service effectively addresses their core problem and delivers both monetary and non-monetary advantages. By presenting these benefits convincingly, you can motivate the customer to step out of their comfort zone and make the decision to move forward in the buying process. Providing concrete evidence and demonstrating how your offering can positively impact their situation will help instill confidence and drive them towards acting.

Types of benefits

As previously discussed, analyzing the types of benefits your product or service can offer to prospective customers is pivotal. The persuasiveness and attractiveness of these benefits directly impact your progress in the sales process.

During your product or service analysis, you can group them into two categories:

o Monetary benefits
o Non-monetary benefits

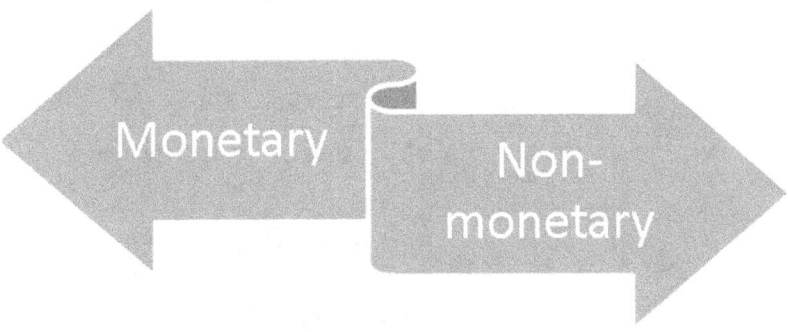

Figure 39 Types of benefits

Non-monetary benefits

As we mentioned previously, there are benefits that are not quantifiable monetarily but that can help to make the purchase. Thus, we must analyze them and include them in our value proposition:

o Fashion
o Trends
o Status
o New corporate demands
o New government regulations
o Brand tastes
o Specific models
o Market tendencies
o Etc.

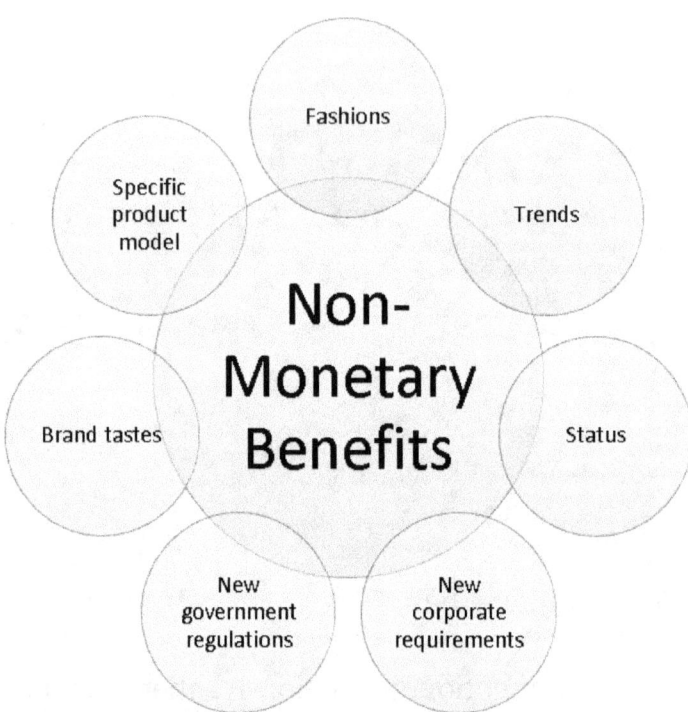

Figure 40 Non-monetary benefits

At this stage, marketing plays a decisive role in positioning the brand of the product or service being offered to create differentiation from competitors and appeal to prospective customers on a non-monetary level.

Monetary benefits

Monetary considerations are indeed the primary and determining step in building trust and internal validation within the client company. It is essential to explain the economic improvements that can be achieved using the product and/or service. These benefits should be clearly and objectively defined, considering the specific circumstances and challenges faced by the client.

In certain instances, I have had to demonstrate to future customers using their information how they can achieve monetary benefits by quantifying them using the product or service, for instance:

- o Savings in productive hours
- o Reduction of unproductive hours
- o Increased sales
- o Personnel savings
- o Equipment optimization
- o Increased production
- o Waste reduction
- o Increased sales margin
- o Increased ROI
- o Increase in customer base.
- o Etc.

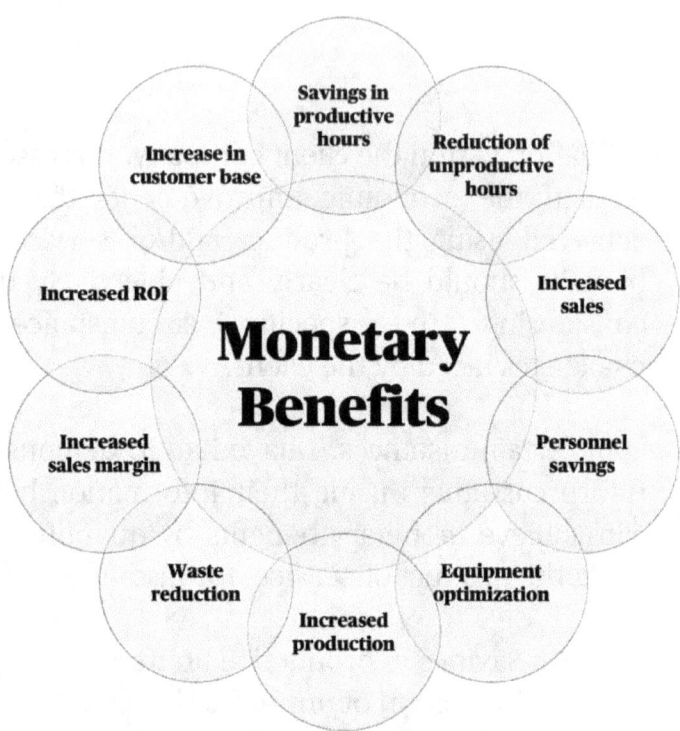

Figure 41 Examples of monetary benefits

Showing the monetary benefits

In certain situations, prospects have asked me to show them a case study that provides concrete examples of how both monetary and non-monetary benefits are obtained, in order to justify the purchase within their company.

In this case, it is important to present a structured scheme of benefits to the prospective customer, starting with the monetary benefits and then highlighting the non-monetary ones. By doing so, you can effectively demonstrate how these benefits complement each other to form a compelling value proposition for the product or service you are offering.

Net present value *calculation*

With a few customers, during the preparation of the value proposition or negotiation stage, I have assisted customers in quantifying the monetary benefits of a project using real data from their company. To achieve this, I have employed the calculation of **net present value (NPV)**. Here is an example with a brief explanation:

The Net Present Value (NPV) is a widely used method in project valuation. In simple terms, it involves converting all future cash flows of a project into their present values by applying a specified financial interest rate.

This method is used to demonstrate the feasibility of moving forward with the purchase of a product or service given the calculated benefits.

$$\text{NPV} = \sum_{x=0}^{n} \frac{R_x}{(1+i)^x}$$

R: Corresponds to the cash flow throughout the period of the project, when purchasing the product and/or service.

n: Corresponds to the duration period of the investment.

i: Discount rate (or rate of return on an investment with a similar risk).

As an example, we will take:

i= 7%
n= 5 years

Item/Year	0	1	2	3	4	5
Revenue		$43.500	$43.500	$43.500	$43.500	$43.500
Initial Investment	-$100.000					
Costs		$5.600	$5.600	$5.600	$5.600	$5.600
Result (R)	-$100.000	$37.900	$37.900	$37.900	$37.900	$37.900

Figure 42 NPV example

$$NPV = \frac{-100.000}{(1+0,07)^0} + \frac{37.900}{(1+0,07)^1} + \frac{37.900}{(1+0,07)^2} + \frac{37.900}{(1+0,07)^3} + \frac{37.900}{(1+0,07)^4} + \frac{37.900}{(1+0,07)^5}$$

$$NPV = 55{,}397.48$$

This calculation indicates that the project, with the purchase of the product and/or service over a 5-year horizon, would yield a net present value of $55,397.48. This positive value suggests that the project is expected to generate a return that exceeds the initial investment when considering the time value of money.

By utilizing *the net present value (NPV) method,* you can effectively demonstrate to your prospective customer the quantifiable monetary benefits they can expect from the project. This allows you to provide concrete evidence of the project's financial viability, which can be presented to both internal stakeholders and external parties who may be interested in the investment. The NPV calculation provides a clear and objective measure of the project's profitability, enabling you to showcase the potential return on investment and substantiate the value proposition to various stakeholders.

NOTE: It is highly recommended to have real data from the prospective customer in order to conduct this type of analysis and assess the benefits obtained with clarity and objectivity.

Additional factors to generate value to the proposal.

There are other key factors that are important to consider in order to differentiate your proposal and create value:

- o *Marketing strategy* as a differentiating element to the value proposition:

  As previously noted, marketing strategy seeks to enhance the attributes of your product or service in the minds of consumers, creating differentiation and positioning against competitors through effective brand building. It is important to note that future customers often prefer to purchase from well-known or recommended brands, as it helps mitigate their risk aversion.

- *Price* as a bet on the value proposition:

  The price of your product or service should be competitive, reflecting the value delivered and creating a sense of paying for the benefits that the customer will receive. It is essential to align the price with the perceived value and benefits that the future customer will derive from your offering.

- *After-sales service and customer service* as a contribution to the value proposition:

  After-sales service and customer service contribute significant value to your proposition, demonstrating the benefits received by current customers and their transferability to future customers. This reduces uncertainty and encourages potential customers to trust and purchase your product or service, even without direct familiarity with your brand and company.

o *Methodology and industry expertise* serve as valuable assets in positioning your service or product:

The specific methodology and skills employed within your industry or sector can be a key differentiating factor. By demonstrating how these translate into tangible benefits, such as time savings or increased revenue, you can effectively showcase the value you bring to the future customer. This highlights your ability to deliver results and sets you apart from competitors who may not possess the same level of industry knowledge and expertise.

Proposal content

The content and form of the proposal to be presented to your future customer may vary depending on the type of sale:

o Direct purchase

o Public tender

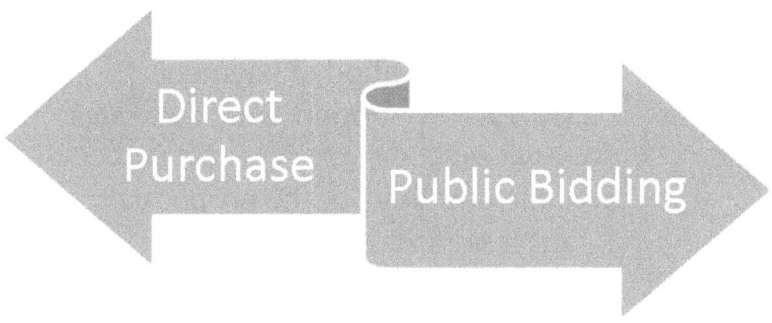

Figure 43 Types of proposals

Direct purchase

When crafting a proposal for a direct purchase, it is essential to emphasize the economic benefits that the customer will gain from using the service or product. The proposal should outline the central problem the customer is facing and present a clear and cohesive narrative that revolves around how the proposed solution addresses and resolves that problem.

The content proposed in this type of direct purchase proposal must contain at least the following basic scheme:

- o Executive summary.
- o Brief description of the company.
- o Technical proposal of the solution or service offered.
- o Detailed benefits.

- o Economic proposal.
- o Type and method of payment.
- o Warranties, support, and after-sales services.
- o Time of validity of the proposal.
- o Success stories.

Executive summary

In this section, it is crucial to include a concise summary of the proposal, outlining the key sections and highlighting the benefits for the client while emphasizing differentiation from the competition.

This summary serves as an executive overview that can be presented to high-level stakeholders, such as owners and directors, who have limited time to review the entire proposal in detail.

Brief description of the company

At this stage, it is important to highlight the company's experience in successfully solving similar problems and the expertise it brings to the proposed solutions. Emphasize the various areas or sectors that the company has effectively addressed, showcasing the breadth and depth of its knowledge and capabilities.

Technical proposal of the solution or service offered.

This section must explain in detail the entire solution of the product or service offered. This must be done in a simple, didactic, and graphic way for the users and the whole client's team to clearly understand it.

Detailed benefits.

In this section you should carve out the benefits that the future customer will gain from using the product or implementing the service.

This section will be key to convince the future customer that the product or service is convenient to be acquired by its company.

Note: For details of which benefits to include see the Types of *Benefits* section

Economic proposal

In this section, it is crucial to provide detailed information about the value and scope of the proposed solution. Include specific details about the service terms, coverage, and duration of the service or use of the product. This clarity helps the future customer understand the extent of the offering and its relevance to their needs.

Type and method of payment

In this section, it is important to specify how the billing and collections will be conducted. Clearly indicate whether the payments will be made in a specific currency, such as US dollars or euros, to avoid any ambiguity. Additionally, outline the billing frequency and payment terms. Specify whether the billing will be monthly, at the beginning of the service, or according to a schedule. Clarify how collections will be carried out, whether it is monthly, every two months, or based on a different interval.

Time of validity of the proposal

In this section, it is important to specify the validity period of the proposal. Clearly state how long the proposal will remain valid, whether it is for one month, six months, or any other specified timeframe.

Warranties, support, and after-sales services

In this section, provide detailed information about the warranties, support, and after-sales services associated with the proposed solution.

Success stories

It is advisable to include a chapter with success stories in order to generate the necessary confidence with the client. This demonstrates that they are not the first to use the service or product and highlights its track record of success.

Public tender

In a proposal for a public tender, the content may vary based on the specific requirements of the future customer. However, common themes typically include:

- o Executive summary of the proposal.

- o Company description and relevant experience.

- o Certificates of financial condition in compliance with tender requirements.

- o Technical proposal outlining the solution or service offered in alignment with tender requirements.

- o Benefit Analysis

o Economic proposal offered in accordance with the requirements of the tender.

o Payment type and method.

o Proposal validity period.

o Guarantees, support, and after-sales services provided.

o Certification of success stories and current customers of the company.

In general, the contents of a proposal for a public tender are similar to those of a private one. However, it is important to carefully consider and address all the technical and economic requirements specified in the bidding rules. The proposal should be designed to meet as many requirements and functionalities as possible as requested by the tender.

Pricing strategy

Understanding the pricing strategy that your company has is key to adding value to your proposal. We will analyze this concept in detail below.

The pricing strategy of a product or service plays a crucial role in the overall value proposition. It is important to consider various alternatives and determine the most suitable pricing approach based on the type of product or service and the company's market strategy. Here are a few examples of pricing strategies:

- o *Price for Basic/Premium Service (Low-Cost Entry Pricing)*: This strategy involves offering a product or service at a low initial price to attract customers, and then charging a higher price for additional features or premium services.

- o Price by service levels (Value-Based Tiered Pricing): This strategy involves offering different levels of service or product configurations to customers, with each tier providing increasing levels of functionality or benefits. Customers can choose a base plan at a lower price and have the option to upgrade to higher tiers with more advanced features or enhanced services.

- o *Price based on the profit obtained (Profit-Based Pricing)*: This strategy involves determining the price of a product or service as a percentage of the profit that the customer is expected to generate from using it.

o *Price per usage (Tiered Pricing with Usage-based Component)*: This pricing strategy involves establishing a base price for the product or service, which covers the essential features or access. In addition to the base price, a variable value is added based on the usage or the number of users who will utilize the system. This approach allows customers to pay for what they actually use or the scale of their usage, ensuring that the pricing aligns with their specific needs and usage requirements.

o *Fixed price per month (Fixed Subscription Pricing)*: This pricing strategy involves setting a fixed value for the product or service regardless of usage. Customers are charged a predetermined amount for a specific period, such as 12 months, regardless of how much they utilize the product or service during that time. This approach provides simplicity and predictability for customers, as they know the exact cost, they will incur over the specified period.

Price analysis for your organization

To enhance your value proposition and facilitate successful negotiations, you must determine if your organization's prices for products and/or services are segmented by country or sector. By understanding the specific needs and market dynamics of different regions or industries, you can tailor your pricing strategy accordingly. This may involve offering discounts or promotions to specific future customers in order to incentivize their purchase and create additional value for them. By customizing your pricing approach, you can demonstrate flexibility and a deep understanding of your customers' unique circumstances, thereby increasing the chances of closing the sale successfully.

Understand your organization.

When crafting your value proposition, it is key to have a comprehensive understanding of your organization's internal dynamics. Familiarize yourself with the different departments, their functions, and how they interact with each other. This knowledge will enable you to streamline the content and gather the necessary information for your proposal effectively.

In some organizations there are review and approval processes for proposals prior to their release. Effective communication and collaboration across departments are of utmost importance here. Adopting an agile approach helps expedite the completion and approval of proposals, especially when dealing with time-sensitive situations like public tenders.

Giving value before calling for action.

A critical factor for the customer before making a purchase decision is to perceive your contribution of value as an expert in your sector. Establishing a connection of trust and showcasing your expertise builds confidence in the customer's mind, and showcases the tangible value contribution that your product or service can offer, for example:

- o *Helping them understand* the problem they must solve today.
- o *Offer a comprehensive understanding of the problem* and present various possible solutions, even if your product or service is not the immediate fit.
- o *Highlight the monetary and non-monetary benefits* they will gain from solving the problem.
- o Offer to test your product and/or service so that they clearly understand the benefits regardless of whether they will move forward or not.
- o Etc.

These actions generate value in advance and confidence to make the sale easier in this sales process or in the following ones you have with your future customer.

Call to action

As the sales process progresses, it becomes clear that motivating customers to make a purchase decision can be challenging. To address this, it's important to prepare and focus on helping and motivating the future customer.

The call to action (CTA) is a powerful technique used to motivate, inspire, empower, and guide the future customer towards taking the desired action in the sales process. It can be employed at various stages of the sales cycle, such as during initial engagement, product demonstrations, or follow-up discussions. A well-crafted and compelling call to action helps create a sense of urgency, encourages the customer to decide, and provides clear instructions on how to proceed.

The key to these motivations is creating a sense of urgency to make a purchase, leveraging the principle of scarcity, and emphasizing the associated benefits of acquiring the product or service. By highlighting the limited availability and positioning it as a unique opportunity, customers are encouraged to act swiftly to avoid missing out on the benefits and satisfaction that come with it. The premise is that if they don't make the purchase, they risk losing the chance to obtain the product or service along with its accompanying advantages and rewards.

Here are some examples of effective call-to-action phrases:

- o "Buy now and start enjoying the benefits..."

- o "If you buy now, we give you a discount of 15%, and you start paying in January of next year..."

- o " Experience the benefits and guaranteed satisfaction of our service today by trying our free trial for one month..."

- o " Why wait any longer? Seize the opportunity to acquire the market's most innovative product today and solve your problem once and for all. Don't miss out on this unique opportunity!...

o " Limited stock available! Don't miss your chance to buy now and start enjoying top-quality products today!"

o Etc.

The list of phrases for a call to action can be extensive and varies depending on the creativity of the seller and the company.

Finally, in my experience, the call to action plays a pivotal role in advancing consultative sales. However, it is important to use it at the right time and when the customer is already convinced or moderately convinced that the product or service can address their central problem or need, and they believe in the associated benefits.

Chapter 7: Negotiate

The negotiation process plays a crucial role in achieving the closure of the agreement during the sales process. It is essential to have a thorough understanding of the negotiation process and be able to effectively control it.

Additionally, it is critical that the future customer does not abandon the acquisition due to bureaucratic hurdles and a slow negotiation process. Therefore, we must ensure that the negotiation process is agile, simple, and clear, minimizing any potential barriers or complexities.

Build relationships of trust

At this stage of the sales process, it is decisive to have already established relationships of trust with both your sponsor and the negotiating team of the future customer. This pre-existing trust will facilitate a smoother negotiation process, as you can build upon the foundation of trust that has already been established. Starting the negotiation process without a pre-existing relationship of trust can lead to potential obstacles or delays in the sale.

Proposal review meetings

After receiving the initial value proposition, the client will review the proposal and schedule a joint review meeting. During this meeting, which marks the formal start of the negotiation process, the client may raise doubts and objections about various aspects of the proposal, including:

- o The technical scope of the solution.

- o The scope of services and service levels provided.

- o Questions about pricing and additional costs.

- o Concerns about the planification and implementation timeline.

- o Doubts regarding the executing team for the project or service.

- o Objections to specific areas of the proposal.

- o Objections related to specific topics such as prices or guarantees.

- o Other miscellaneous concerns.

For each of the issues and objections raised during the negotiation process, it is important to be prepared with thoughtful and persuasive responses.

The details of the negotiations and objections will be reviewed below.

What is being negotiated?

In all the negotiation processes that I have participated in prior to closing a sale, there are always key elements that are negotiated, for example:

- o Price of the product or service.
- o Additional functionality in the case of products.
- o Scope of services (territory, functionality, etc.).
- o Duration of the contract.
- o Installation deadlines.
- o Product or service start dates.
- o Type and form of payments.
- o Currency of payment.
- o Volume discount.

o Exclusivity of use.
o Brand reproduction.
o Advertising for use of the product or service.
o Early departure clauses.
o Fines for non-compliance.
o Agreement Frameworks and Levels of Specific Services (SLA, MSA).

The previous list is referential, and can vary from client to client, but in general, these are the concepts that are most repeated in a negotiation process.

Each mentioned can potentially trigger a negotiation during the sales process. In general, the negotiations can be grouped into three main areas:

o Technical Negotiations

o Business and Economic Negotiations

o Legal Negotiations

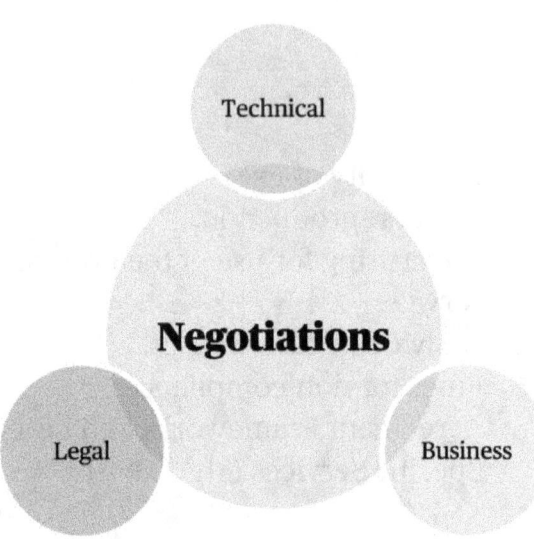

Figure 44 Types of negotiations

During the sales process, negotiations and objections can indeed arise in the three areas mentioned, and the order in which these negotiations are approached may vary depending on the type of client and their specific needs and concerns.

Maintaining a sequential order from technical to business, and finally to legal and regulatory aspects is advisable during the negotiation process. This ensures a structured approach and addresses different aspects of the proposal in a logical manner, involving relevant stakeholders from each area, as shown here:

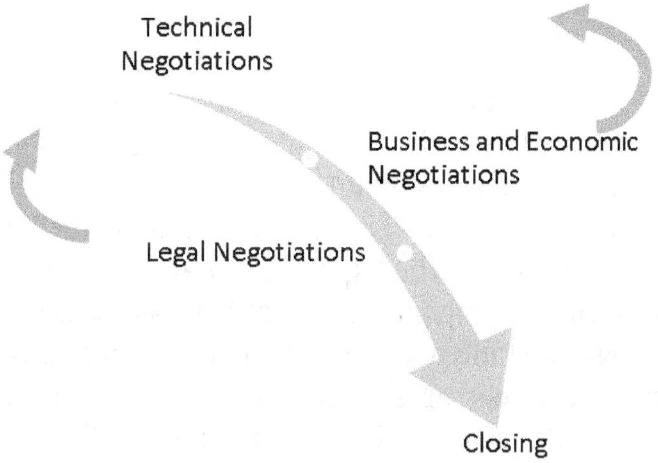

Technical
Negotiations

Business and Economic
Negotiations

Legal Negotiations

Closing

Figure 45 Negotiation process

In clients where the sponsor's influence may not be widespread or there are multiple departments involved in the purchase process, an iterative negotiation approach can be beneficial. This means that certain aspects, such as technical issues, can be revisited and discussed again during the negotiation process, even when addressing legal or regulatory matters. This flexibility allows for a more comprehensive and collaborative negotiation process.

Never start the negotiation with the closing price

This concept of not starting the negotiation with a fixed final price, but rather with a referential value or price range, is a valuable lesson learned through trial and error. By doing so, you maintain flexibility to accommodate the specific needs of the future customer in solving their problem. As the negotiation progresses and additional agreements are made, such as increasing service levels or adding guarantees or early departure clauses, it allows for a more comprehensive and tailored agreement. This iterative approach ensures that the final price reflects the overall value and scope of the service or product.

As mentioned above, it is important to understand during the negotiation process that the price must reflect the contribution of value and benefits that you provide to the client and that this aligns with the client's willingness to pay.

Understanding "NOs" as objections

In every purchase process, the prospect will always have two perspectives regarding the purchase of the product and/or service:

o One that reinforces your arguments and favors purchasing the product or service, **"Yes buy."**

o The other one that includes the set of **objections, "Do not buy"**.

Since these scenarios are common in all sales processes, it is essential to be prepared to strengthen the **buying vision** and address any **objections** that may arise in the prospect's mind to encourage them to make the purchase.

Objections not to buy can arise at any stage of the sales cycle, whether it's during the initial contact, product or service presentation, proposal presentation, or when closing the contract. Some examples include:

o "I don't want to proceed as I don't need it."

o "It's very expensive, I have no budget."

o "It's not a good time of the year."

o "I need to validate it with the owners."

o "I do not agree with the form of payment stated in the contract. "

- o "We work differently and the service and/or product does not adapt to the needs we have."

- o "Let me think about it, I'll call you later."

- o Etc.

Do not be discouraged by receiving objections or hearing "**NO**" as a response. It is a normal part of the sales process and every salesperson encounter objection. Objections and resistance may arise depending on the client, industry, and location. It's important not to take objections personally, but rather approach them with a problem-solving mindset and a determination to find a mutually beneficial solution.

Based on experience in the sector, country, and specific product/service, it is possible to establish metrics indicating the average number of negative responses required to obtain a positive sale. For instance, it may take around ten negative responses on average to secure a single "**Yes**".

This process is like when you look for a new job, you will have interviews and they will tell you after several important interviews that you are hired.

The higher the number of "NOs" in your sales process, the closer you are to reaching the desired "YES" and advancing in the sales process. As you progress, you will start to understand the percentages of "NOs" required to ultimately secure a "YES" and close a sale. For example, you may find that you need an 80% rejection rate to eventually obtain a successful sale, as depicted in the following figure.

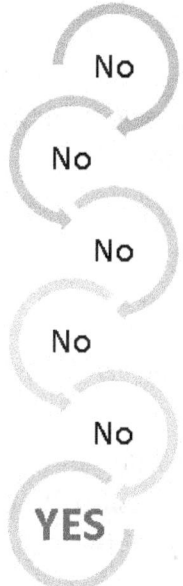

Figure 46 Cycle to achieve moving forward.

Negotiation follow-up

To maintain control over the sales process, it is crucial to monitor the negotiation process across all the areas we have discussed. Each negotiated issue has the potential to bring about significant modifications to the proposal and solution presented to the client.

Effective follow-up of the negotiation requires a comprehensive understanding of the sales process. This allows you to prioritize and update the status of agreed and pending issues, ensuring a systematic progression in the negotiations. By maintaining a global perspective, you can track the overall progress, address any outstanding matters, and ensure that the negotiation moves forward in an organized and efficient manner.

Objections management

Effectively managing objections, which is just handling "Nos" as answers, is a vital skill in sales. By understanding the underlying reasons behind objections and preparing persuasive responses, you can turn a "no" into a "yes". Rather than viewing objections as roadblocks, see them as opportunities to address concerns and provide valuable information. Analyzing objections and preparing persuasive responses allows you to address customer concerns, demonstrate expertise, and build trust.

One way to determine if the objection is real or just a temporary mistrust of the product and/or service or the company, is to ask questions such as the following:

- o Does our proposed solution align with your needs and address the problem you are looking to solve?

- o Putting aside the price aspect, does our proposal meet your requirements and offer the anticipated benefits in solving your problem?

- o How do you perceive the monetary benefits that you would gain from utilizing this product and/or service?

- o What do you think about the non-monetary benefits?

- o In economic terms, does the price fit your budget?

- o What specific aspect would you like to see included in the proposal to move forward with it?

- o Etc.

By analyzing the responses from prospective customers, you can identify both the barriers that are preventing them from progressing in the sales process and the underlying reasons behind their objections.

Based on my sales experience, objections can be classified into at least three categories:

- o Technical objections

- o Business and economic objections

- o Legal objections

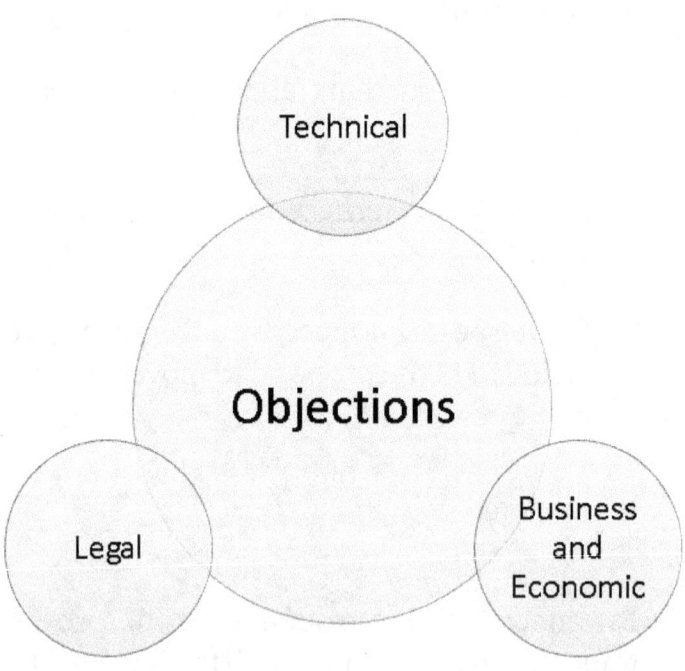

Figure 47 Types of objections

Note: *There may be more particular types of objections such as environmental, political, etc. depending on the company, sector, and target market.*

Overcoming obstacles

To effectively manage objections, it is significant to have a comprehensive and concise list of the objections that prospects commonly raise. Once identified, it is essential to develop a corresponding set of proposals and strategies aimed at addressing and minimizing these objections.

Certainly, having a structured approach can greatly assist in managing objections and navigating the sales process. Here are some tactical steps you can follow:

1. *Define in a document or a presentation* all the points that do not allow the client to move forward with the purchase.

2. With the knowledge you already have of the customer and your product or service, propose an *alternative or solution* for each of their objections.

3. If there is an objection that cannot be resolved, it is best to address it honestly and

transparently with the client at this stage of the process. It is important to avoid creating *false expectations* and instead focus on finding alternative solutions or addressing any limitations openly.

4. *Schedule* a follow-up meeting with the prospective customer after conducting the analysis to address and discuss the objections raised.

5. Finally, be prepared for the objection handling process to occur multiple times as the prospective customer evaluates their decision and is ready to move on to the next step.

This process of managing objections can be iterative, starting with addressing objections from the technical field, followed by objections from the business and economic aspects, and concluding with objections related to the legal aspects.

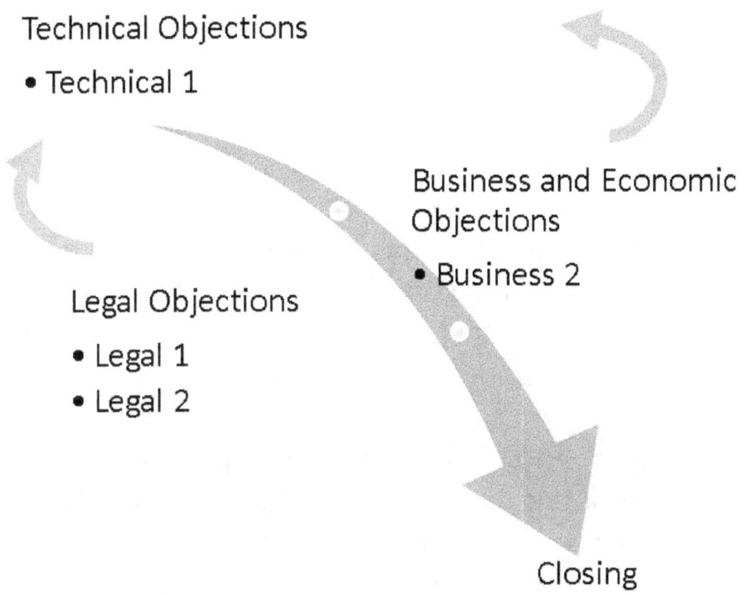

Technical Objections
• Technical 1

Business and Economic Objections
• Business 2

Legal Objections
• Legal 1
• Legal 2

Closing

Figure 48 Following the objections process.

This is an example of objection management that I use in this process:

Date	Type	Objections	Proposals	Status
10/10/2023	Technical	I need a monthly data report	A monthly report with 10 items of your choice can be added within the scope.	**Accepted**
20/11/2023	Business and Economic	I cannot pay the full amount of the contract at the beginning.	Pay in 12 installments	**Under review**
05/12/2023	Legal	We do not want exclusivity of use of the product, so we can have others in use at the same time.	Non-exclusivity of use is granted	**Pending**

Figure 49 Analysis of objections

183

Final negotiations

In this final negotiation, it is important to consider factors that are relevant to the future customer in order to achieve the closure of the process. While price is often a consideration, it is equally important to highlight the benefits and functions that can help reduce or optimize their processes.

As I have observed, in companies with multiple negotiating areas, it is common for each department to assert their bargaining power during the final negotiations. They may seek to demonstrate their contribution to the process and influence the terms of the purchase agreement. In this stage, it is important to address any final objections that arise, ensuring that all parties feel heard, and their concerns are adequately addressed. These are examples, of some final objections:

- o The Legal area may raise objections and add final clauses related to the scenario of an early exit from the contract.

- o The IT department may raise objections and propose the inclusion of key performance indicators (KPIs) or service level agreements (SLAs).

- The end user may introduce a final request for a new functionality or special service to be included in the solution.

- Etc.

In order to successfully navigate the final negotiation and address these last objections and requests, it is crucial to be well-prepared. This involves thoroughly analyzing each objection or request, understanding its implications, and formulating appropriate responses or counteroffers. It may require collaborating with different teams or departments within your organization to assess the feasibility and impact of these requests.

Overall, in these negotiations it is essential to explore alternative solutions and think creatively to find mutually beneficial outcomes. While you may not always be able to lower the price, offering additional services or functionalities can be a valuable way to add value to the proposal without compromising your internal costs significantly. By identifying and highlighting these additional benefits, you can provide the customer with an attractive proposition that addresses their needs and goes beyond their initial expectations. This approach can create a win-win situation, where both parties feel satisfied with the outcome of the negotiation.

Chapter 8: Monitoring and Controlling

T sales process is not a one-time activity, but rather an ongoing practice that should be ingrained in your sales routine. Monitoring and controlling the sales process is essential for advancing and accelerating sales. It provides strategic and tactical visibility, allowing informed decision-making and proactive action. By adopting this habit, you ensure that you have a strategic and tactical understanding of your potential customers and the actions needed to move them forward in the sales process.

The importance of follow-up

Effective follow-up with prospective customers is a key factor in driving successful sales. By understanding their needs and staying engaged with their current situation, you can navigate the sales process effectively and increase the likelihood of closing the deal.

I would like to share a story about a prospective customer I will refer to as James. I had been following James for quite some time because I believed he fit the profile of someone who would benefit from the product I was offering.

James, the owner of a company with subsidiaries in two cities, had a specific need that our product could address. After reviewing the product and understanding its functionality, James agreed with the analysis of the benefits he could achieve. We offered him a pilot, but he was already convinced that the product was the solution he needed. Unfortunately, the COVID-19 pandemic struck, forcing James to cancel all purchases and temporarily halt operations.

After some time, I continued to periodically follow up with James to stay updated on his business and whether his needs had evolved. Each time, he expressed that it wasn't the right time yet. However, one day, I sent him an email informing him of the updated commercial conditions and a special discount available if he made the purchase this year. To my delight, James responded stating "Let's talk, now is the time" and expressing his interest in moving forward with the purchase.

After two years of initial contact and consistent follow-up, the sale finally got completed.

As we have seen in the previous example, sometimes it is necessary to wait for the right time because there are factors that may have delayed the purchase of the future customer at the right time, such as:

- *No budget*: The prospect did not have the budget in the year the offer was made, but now they have enough funds.

- *Non-relevant*: The impact of the central problem was not yet relevant to the business, but in this new scenario it is.

- *Non-Beneficial*: Initially, the benefits were not compelling enough for the customer to proceed with the purchase process. However, after adjusting input costs and services, the feasibility of the purchase has significantly improved.

- *Non-priority*: The priorities of the company have shifted since the initial contact and the first value offering. As a result, they are now ready to move forward with the purchase.

- o *Change in stakeholders*: The change in ownership or management of the company has resulted in a renewed interest in solving the need and central problem with the product being offered.

- o *New need*: A new need has arisen, which did not exist at the time when the product or service was initially presented.

Figure 50 Factors to delaying purchase.

What factors are key to moving the process forward?

From my point of view, it is possible to identify some key factors to see if the future customer is moving forward in the process. Some of these characteristics to analyze include:

- o **Need**: There is a need or problem that my product or service can address.

- o **Trust**: The client trusts you and the proposal you sent.

- o **Resolution**: The prospect believes that the product or service can help resolve their needs or problems.

- o **Benefits**: The benefits offered align with the prospect's purchasing decision.

- o **Budget**: Budget is available to make the purchase.

- o **Conditions**: There is agreement with the conditions of purchase for the product or service.

- o **Time**: The timing is appropriate to make the purchase.

- o **External Factors**: There are some external factors that can speed up the purchase.

- o **Internal Factors**: There is an internal factor in the company that could potentially hinder the purchase.

The following depicts the factors in a graphical form.

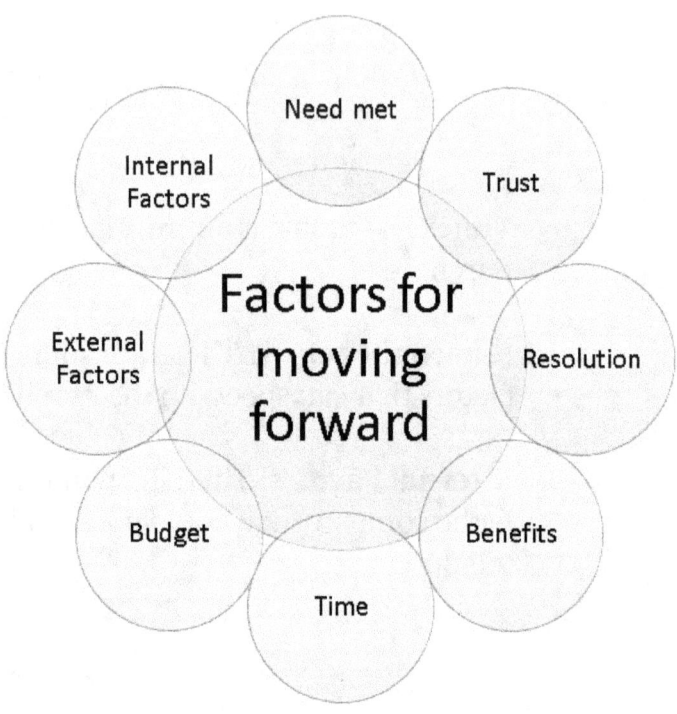

Figure 51 Factors to move forward with the sale.

By analyzing all these factors, it allows for a detailed assessment of each prospective customer and enables a focused effort to determine which area of the sales process needs strengthening in order to persuade the prospect to move forward.

Analysis of the monitoring and controlling process

One key to achieving sales success is to conduct a regular analysis of follow-up and control of your prospective customers (potential customers and prospects) throughout the entire sales process. This analysis can be performed on a daily or weekly basis, assessing the status of each prospect, updating their progress, evaluating the market situation, and determining the necessary actions to advance to the next stage.

It is important to regularly analyze your sales processes at a global level, at least once a week. This allows for strategic and tactical planning, setting priorities, addressing internal matters, and fulfilling commitments made to prospective customers. Developing this habit is essential in your new role, and utilizing tools described in the following points can greatly assist in this endeavor.

To review the process, it is possible to use a schema that shows the status of future customers in the sales process at a general level such as the following:

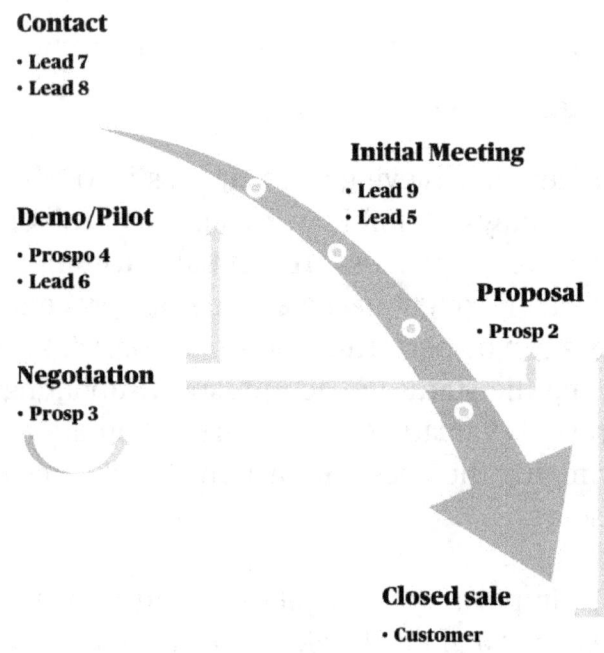

Contact
· Lead 7
· Lead 8

Initial Meeting
· Lead 9
· Lead 5

Demo/Pilot
· Prospo 4
· Lead 6

Proposal
· Prosp 2

Negotiation
· Prosp 3

Closed sale
· Customer

5252 Monitoring and controlling the sales conflict.

As shown in the previous diagram, the sales process is not always linear. There may be instances where customers need to "return to a previous stage" or remain in the same stage for further actions. For example, a negotiation might require an adjusted proposal based on a new agreement or a new demonstration for the company's board. The arrows in the diagram represent these returns or continuations within the sales process.

Another way to analyze the status of the sales process is to detail each of the prospects you have at each stage as shown below:

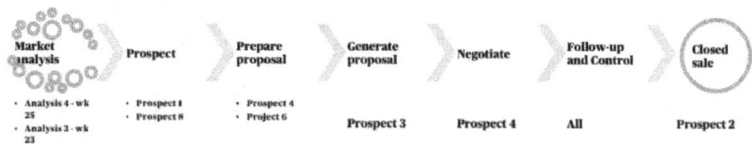

Figure 53 Vision of the monitoring and controlling process.

The above scheme provides a comprehensive and strategic view of the sales funnel (pipeline) for each of your future customers (potential customers and prospects), allowing you to identify their stage in the sales process. This information is determining in prioritizing and allocating resources effectively, ensuring that each customer receives the appropriate attention and support at their specific stage of the funnel.

Additionally, we can build a table showing a more tactical detail of the current situation and the next actions to take for each prospect as such:

Type	Phase	Actions taken	Upcoming actions	Status Sale
Prospect 1	Closing the sale	11/10/2022 Contract signed.	Start of service 1/11/2022	Closed
Prospect 2	Proposal	10/09/2022 Preparing the economic and technical offer.	30/09/2022 Proposal submission	In progress
Prospect 3	Negotiation	10/11/2022 Meeting with the customer: conclusion requests a 10% discount on the product.	20/11/2022 Meeting with customer to make a counterproposal, the issue is being analyzed today by the Commercial Director.	Pending

Figure 54 Detail of monitoring and controlling.

Note: Status and Actions may be adjusted based on the client's industry, market, and policies.

The two key aspects of monitoring and controlling are to provide a *roadmap* for focused efforts and issue resolution with other areas, as well as to differentiate and prioritize prospects who are ready to advance in the purchasing decision from those who are not.

Prioritization of future customers

As we saw in *Chapter 4 - Prospecting*, it is important to periodically review and reassess the prioritization parameters in order to refocus our actions on new prospects that may have emerged.

The variables to review are:

- o *Market share*
- o *Categorization*
- o *Territorial coverage*

If any of these items have changed and thus rearranged the prioritization list. We will detect it quickly, for example:

- o *Change in territorial coverage*: If a prospect has transitioned from regional coverage to global coverage.

- o *Change in market share*: if the market share went from 5% to 35% then this becomes relevant.

- o *Change in the client's company*: If there is a change in ownership and it has gone from being a conservative company to an innovative one.

- o Etc.

Current customer tracking

An important lesson I learned during the sales cycles is:

"It is easier to sell additional products or services to an existing customer than to acquire a new customer."

Therefore, it is important to validate with your current customers whether they have any new needs that can be addressed by your current or future products through *cross-selling or additional sales.*

In addition, staying in regular contact with your current customers can facilitate new sales opportunities. By maintaining communication on a monthly or periodic basis, you can assess the satisfaction and performance of your service or product, gather valuable feedback through after-sales service, and identify any unmet needs that may require additional coverage or solutions. The following list of current customers can serve as a guide for your follow-up efforts:

Customer	Type	Need	Product and service	Last meeting
Company 1	Innovator	Need 1	Product A	01-2023: No change needed.
Company H	Leader	Need 1 and 2	Service 2	04-2022: Company is in the process of getting restructured. Possible contact change in one month
Company J	Follower	Need 3	Product 3	05-2023: New need found during presentation.

Figure 55 Analysis of current customers

Note: If any of the current customers have a new requirement that needs to be addressed, it should be entered into the normal sales process for tracking the respective sale.

It is important to note that in this type of consultative sales, the follow-up and contact with the client play a crucial role in advancing the sales process. The actions you carry out will be decisive on whether or not you achieve your sales objective.

In consultative sales, simply relying on marketing efforts is not enough to convert an interested prospect into a customer. While marketing plays a crucial role in generating leads and creating awareness, the sales process is where the real conversion happens. It is of utmost importance to apply the sales process in detail and control each step, as previously mentioned in other chapters, to maximize the chances of success.

Signs indicating that the process is moving forward.

It is challenging to be absolutely certain if a customer will make a purchase. However, there are certain signs and indicators that can help you gauge their willingness to buy. Some of these signs include:

- o The future customer spontaneously asks for:
  - o The sales process
  - o Benefits
  - o Price
  - o Features
  - o Detail of the implementation of the product and/or service.
  - o Guarantees
  - o After-sales service
  - o Etc.

- o The future customer is willing to discuss the specifics of the closing and contract terms.

- o The future customer actively participates in streamlining the sales process and demonstrates a willingness to advance in the closing. They contribute to new ideas and provide their perspective to reach agreements on key issues.

Chapter 9: Closing the Sale

The process of closing the sale is a crucial stage in achieving the signing of the agreement. By directing the entire process effectively, you can address any remaining objections, clarify terms and conditions, and guide the customer towards making a final commitment.

My first closing of a sale

I still vividly recall the moment when I achieved my first successful sales closure. It was the culmination of persistent efforts and continuous iterations in the sales process. The memories of my journey and the lessons learned flooded my mind. It brought me immense joy and a sense of accomplishment, as I realized that the seemingly insurmountable goal, I had set for myself had finally been conquered. It was a gratifying experience, akin to reaching the summit of a mountain after a challenging ascent.

The entire experience of closing the first sale was immensely gratifying, as it not only marked the achievement of my goal in entering the world of sales but also allowed me to gain a deeper understanding of the process involved in securing future sales.

Achieving the first sale is not only a significant milestone but also a boost of optimism and validation for all the hard work invested in the sales process. It serves as a catalyst for further success, setting the tone for future sales endeavors. It provides an opportunity to reflect on the entire process, identifying areas for improvement and making necessary adjustments. By analyzing the strengths and weaknesses observed, it becomes possible to refine the sales approach and enhance the overall effectiveness in engaging with prospective customers. This valuable feedback paves the way for pursuing the next prospects with renewed confidence and an improved sales strategy.

The process does not end until the contract is signed.

When a future customer expresses their intention to purchase and their determination to move forward, it signifies progress in the sales process. However, it's important to note that the journey is not yet complete. The process reaches its conclusion only when both parties have signed the contract or agreement to acquire the service and/or product.

During my sales process, I have encountered situations where we have successfully navigated multiple stages of the negotiation. We have reached the point where the contract is drafted, and there is even a verbal agreement from the customer. Everything seems to be in place for signing the deal. However, despite our best efforts, we may not close the sale. These may stem from external factors such as the impact of the pandemic, or internal issues like financial difficulties or budget constraints.

If any of these situations arise during any of the closing stages, it is important to maintain professionalism and composure. Instead of showing anger or frustration towards the future customer, express gratitude for their consideration and thank them cordially. Keep the door open for future opportunities, as circumstances can change, and there may be a possibility to revisit the conversation and move forward with the sale at a later time.

In situations where the sale does not proceed despite reaching the final stage, it is important to acknowledge that both parties have invested time and effort in the process. It is a shared loss, and no one benefits from not signing the contract.

Contract and signature for closing

The drafting and signing of the contract are the final steps in the sales process and signify the completion of the negotiation.

During the contract drafting and negotiation stage, it is common for objections and concerns to arise, both related to the content of the contract and its legal implications. These objections can be raised by either party involved in the sale. To ensure a smooth and satisfactory process, it is advisable to involve the lawyers or legal representatives from both the selling company and the future customer.

Model contract

During contract negotiations, standard contracts can be customized based on the negotiations and recommendations of lawyers from both the selling company and the client. The goal is to address specific requirements, concerns, and legal considerations while reaching a fair agreement. Lawyers play a crucial role in reviewing and finalizing the contract to ensure it is legally sound and that it protects the rights of both parties.

Why do we fail sometimes in closing a sale?

There are several common factors that can contribute to the failure to close a sale, including:

o Lack of trust: The prospect may not trust you, the product, or the company enough to make a purchase.

o Failure to identify the central problem and/or needs: You may have failed to understand and address the core problem and needs of the prospect.

o Lack of connection or trust-building: The sales process may have lacked a strong connection or relationship of trust with the prospect.

o Lack of empathy: You may have failed to empathize with the prospect's problem and needs. Consultative sales rely on trust and empathy to sell products and services.

o Insufficient value proposition: The prospect may not have been convinced that your product or service effectively solves their problem and provides value.

o Perceived lack of value: The prospect may not have perceived the value generated by the product or service in relation to its price, features, and benefits.

Closing a sale

Formally, the sale is considered closed when both parties sign the contract or agreement for the purchase or use of the product and/or service. At that moment, the prospect officially becomes your new customer.

Chapter 10: A Retrospective of the Sale Process

When the sales process has been completed with the signing of a contract for a product or service, it is essential to conduct a retrospective analysis from various perspectives. This analysis helps determine which aspects of the process were executed effectively and identifies areas that require improvement for future customers.

Adjusting the sales process

The duration of the sales process is measured from the initial contact with a potential customer until the point of conversion, where they make a purchase and become a customer.

Through multiple iterations, it has been observed that the sales process for specific services tends to have longer durations compared to that of a product. In addition, they can vary significantly across sectors, niche markets, and countries. Furthermore, even within the same industry, different companies and individual sellers may experience variations in their sales cycle times. It is thus important to consider these variations in sales times when estimating future sales.

The modifications and adjustments to the sales process should be made based on feedback from prospects and potential customers. By closely analyzing their responses, objections, and behaviors throughout the sales cycle, you can identify areas for improvement and make necessary changes to increase sales closings and reduce the overall duration of the process. Continuous iteration, feedback gathering, and refinement of the sales process are vital for achieving optimal results and adapting to the evolving needs and preferences of your target audience.

Customer impressions

It is important to gather the customer's impressions about the sales process from various perspectives, including:

General topics

o   Internal analysis of the sales process
o   Agility in the process

- Simplicity of the process
- Topics for improvement
- Highlights of the process

Contacts and presentations

- Which topics can be highlighted and improved from the initial contacts?
- Did the topics covered in the demonstrations, pilots or process presentations seem important?

- Which topics were missing to detail or comment on during the early stages of the process?

Proposals and negotiations

- What content did you find relevant to the proposal, and what was missing or needed to be added that was later incorporated?

- During the negotiation for the signing of the contract, which process would you highlight, and which topics did you find most complex to address?

Closing and signing

o   What did you think of the standard contract used for closing?

o   Did the timeline for the legal review and contract closure seem reasonable, or did it exceed your initial expectations?

If, after conducting a detailed analysis of this feedback, you find that your sales process is overly complex, slow, or if your closing rate is very low, it is likely that you will need to improve certain aspects of the process. Let's explore some key points to consider:

Improvement suggestions for the sales process

With the information collected both internally and externally, valuable insights can be gained to make improvements at each stage of the sales process. These improvements will benefit all future customers by enhancing the effectiveness and efficiency of the sales journey, for example:

- o *Improving response times* for contract review.
- o *Enhancing the analysis* and response to objections.
- o *Streamlining the preparation* of proposals and contracts.
- o *Enhancing presentations, pilots, and demonstrations.*
- o *Simplifying and expediting* the contracting process once the decision to move forward has been made.

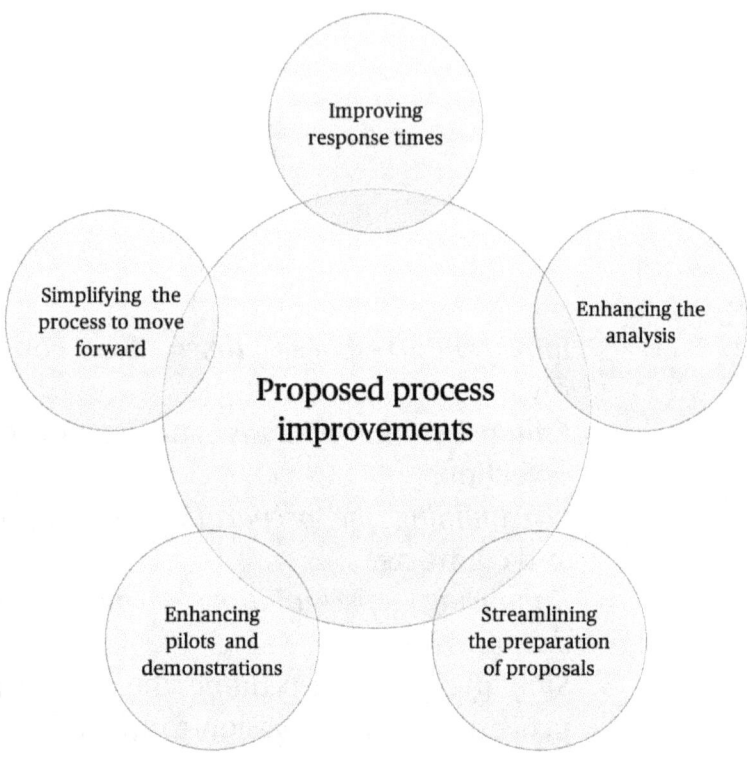

Figure 56 Proposed process improvements.

As we have previously discussed, optimizing the time that future customers spend in the sales process is crucial for closing the sale successfully. To achieve this, it is important to consider internal proposals that streamline the process while maintaining its content and depth. These improvements can be implemented after thorough iterations, gaining a comprehensive understanding of the market and the profile of future customers. Among the improvements to be raised we can find:

- o *Streamline the preparation process for demonstrations and presentations* by predefining all necessary elements beforehand.

- o *Accelerate pilot* implementation and project timelines to showcase additional benefits more effectively.

- o *Expedite the preparation of proposals* to provide prompt and agile responses to future customers.

- o *Predefine proposals that highlight the benefits* of using the product or service, enabling quick delivery to the customer.

- o *Establish predefined agreements* and standard contracts for different contracting modalities to reduce review times and increase sales closings.

Simplifying the negotiation process

To optimize the negotiation process, it is crucial to analyze if it is excessively lengthy or complex for the future customer. This can be done by reviewing historical closing processes and identifying the aspects that are most commonly negotiated by customers. By understanding these patterns, you can proactively prepare and address those specific aspects during the negotiation.

Additionally, it is beneficial to identify any parameters or order in the negotiation that tend to prevail in the consultative sales process. For example, you can determine if technical aspects are typically negotiated first, followed by price discussions, and then business and legal matters.

Characteristics of a salesman

After gaining extensive experience in various sales processes, I have identified a set of essential characteristics that every seller must cultivate in consultative sales to increase their chances of closing a sale. Among these I can highlight:

- o *Being an effective communicator:* possess the skill to explain the benefits and functionality of the product or service clearly and persuasively in a simple and easily understandable manner.

- o *Listen and understand effectively:* The ability to actively listen and comprehend customer needs and requirements.

- o *Confidence in their abilities:* Having confidence in oneself and the product/service being sold, and effectively conveying that confidence to the prospect.

- o *Perseverance:* Being persistent in overcoming objections and obstacles to move the customer towards making a purchase.

- o *Flexibility:* Being adaptable and responsive to changes or requests from the customer, and quickly adjusting proposals and strategies as needed.

- o *Expertise in the field:* Acquiring in-depth knowledge and expertise beyond just the product/service being sold.

o *Building trust relationships:* Fostering trust and rapport with potential customers through effective communication and relationship-building skills.

o *Problem-solving:* Analyzing and proposing creative solutions to business problems that align with the product/service being offered.

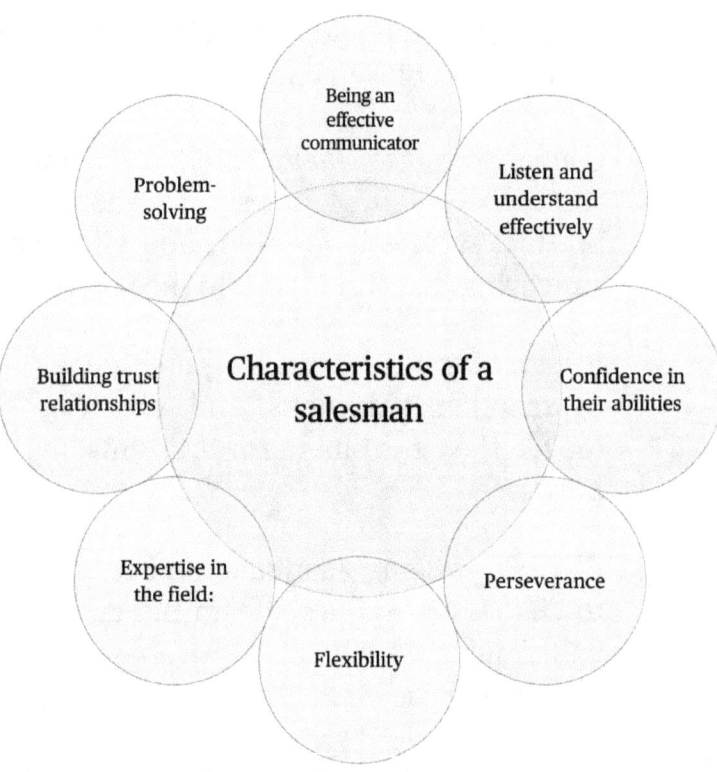

Figure 57 Essential characteristics of a salesman

From Engineering to Sales

Chapter 11: Sales Forecast

Sales forecasting is essential for any company as it enables the projection of income over time, facilitates operational sizing, and aids in planning for future expenses. Additionally, it provides investors with valuable insights into the company's current situation and future prospects.

Probability of closing of sale

Before diving into the sales forecast process, it is crucial to grasp the concept of the probability of closing a sale. This understanding lays the foundation for estimating future sales over a given period.

The probability of success in a sale is determined by evaluating the progress made in the sales process. As the sales process unfolds, certain milestones or stages are reached, indicating the increasing likelihood of closing the sale:

- o have a 10% chance of success in closing a sale, it means that, on average, out of 10 prospects in the sales process, you can expect to close one [1] sale.

This probability of sale can vary depending on various factors such as the sector in which you operate, customer preferences, market conditions, economic factors, geographical location, and the specific product or service you are selling.

In consultative sales, the closing rates can vary significantly depending on the sector and market complexity. It's not uncommon to see closing rates ranging from 20% to 30% in certain sectors where the sales process is more streamlined, and the value proposition is clear. However, in complex markets or industries where the decision-making process is intricate and involves multiple stakeholders, the closing rates can be lower, potentially around 10% or even less.

The demand for specific products or services can fluctuate throughout the year, influenced by factors such as seasons, holidays, or industry-specific trends. As a result, the probability of closing a sale can vary accordingly. For example, during the summer season when the demand for certain products or services is high, the conversion rate may be around 20% as customers are actively seeking those offerings. On the other hand, during the winter season when demand may be lower, the conversion rate may decrease to around 10%. Taking an average across the year, you can estimate an overall conversion rate of approximately 15%.

Another crucial consideration is the composition of your prospect list. The mix of prospects you engage with can have a significant impact on your probability of success. If your list consists mainly of innovative prospects who are open to new ideas and willing to take risks, your probability of closing a sale tends to increase. On the other hand, if your list is composed primarily of conservative prospects who are resistant to change or prefer traditional approaches, your probability of success may decrease.

In conclusion, having the ability to analyze and assess your own probability of closing a sale is of utmost importance. By thoroughly evaluating your iterations of the sales process, you can gather valuable insights and data to inform your future sales strategies. This analysis allows you to identify patterns, strengths, weaknesses, and areas for improvement in your sales approach.

Average selling price

An important factor to consider in future sales forecasts is determining the average selling price.

This metric is calculated by dividing the total sales revenue by the quantity of products or services sold. For example:

If you sold 100 products for a total of $100,000, your average selling price would be $1,000 per unit.

How to estimate future sales

The process of estimating your future sales will be based on variables such as:

- o *Previous Experience:* Your previous experience in sales, including knowledge of the product, competitors, and sales techniques, can give you an advantage in the sales process.

- o *Market situation:* The current state of the market, country, and sector can impact your sales forecast. Economic fluctuations, industry trends, and market conditions can influence the timing and conversion rates of your sales process.

o *Prospects:* Analyzing your current list of prospects and their profiles as previously mentioned is imperative. The quality and alignment of your prospects with your product or service offering can affect your sales closures.

o *Probability of closing the sale*: Your current probability of closing a sale, which is influenced by factors such as your sales skills, prospect engagement, objection handling, and competitive positioning, should be considered when estimating future sales.

o *New products*: The introduction of new products in the market, especially those that directly compete with or complement your offerings, can impact your sales estimates. Assess the potential market impact of these new products on your sales performance.

o *Marketing Strategies:* The effectiveness of your marketing activities, such as advertising, promotions, lead generation, and brand awareness, can influence your sales forecast.

o *Competitors:* Analyze your competitors' strategies, market position, pricing, and value propositions. Understanding their strengths and weaknesses can help you anticipate market dynamics and adjust your sales forecast accordingly.

o *Prices and Costs:* Fluctuation of the prices and costs of your product and / or service.

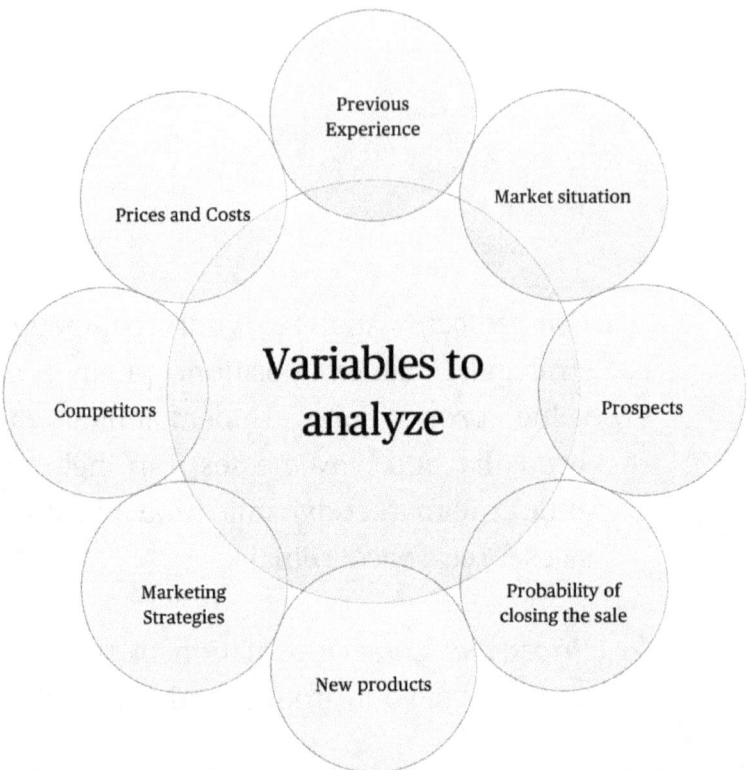

Figure 58 Variables for sales forecast

There are several methods available for making sales forecasts, including statistical analysis, machine learning techniques, historical income analysis, and analyzing the current and projected sales process.

We will review two methods that can be used easily and quickly.

Sales projection as a funnel analysis

Since you keep track and control of your funnel through the sales process and have an estimated calculation of sales probabilities and average sales price, you can estimate your future sales as follows:

If you have twenty prospects in your funnel, with an average conversion rate of 30% per year and an average selling price of $2,000, your sales projection would be:

20 prospects x 30% conversion rate x $2,000 average selling price = $12,000.

Sales projection as revenue percentage

One of the quickest methods of estimating sales projection is to determine sales based on the share of revenue and trends from the past, and then projecting future sales with consideration to factors such as the current economic conditions of the country or market, market preferences and trends, activities of competitors, and other relevant factors.

Based on the historical data provided, it can be inferred that new sales accounted for approximately 25% of the company's total revenue in the past three years. This means that if the company had an annual revenue of 1 million dollars, the new sales generated during that period would amount to 250,000 dollars (25% of 1 million dollars). This information can be used as a reference point to estimate future sales based on the company's revenue projections.

Now, if this year historical sales are weighted 5% more this year due to economic uncertainty and other factors, the factor for new sales as a percentage of income would be 30%. Therefore, if the projected revenue for the year is 1 million dollars, the estimated new sales required would be 300,000 dollars (30% of 1 million dollars).

It's important to note that this method assumes a certain level of regularity and stability in sales patterns and past trends. However, external factors and market conditions can influence actual sales performance, so it's always advisable to consider multiple factors and conduct a comprehensive analysis when making sales projections.

Sales quota

A sales quota is a specific monetary target that the sales department or individual salespeople aim to achieve within a defined period of time. The sales quota can be set on a monthly, quarterly, semi-annual, or annual basis, depending on the company's sales cycle and objectives.

Additionally, in sales quota systems, we often include the provision for incentive payments based on the achievement of partial or total goals. These incentives can take the form of bonuses, commissions, or other types of rewards. For example:

- For quota attainment:

  - Achieving 85% of the sales quota may result in a bonus of one year's salary.
  - A bonus of two salaries per year is paid by achieving 95% of the sales.
  - Exceeding the sales quota by 105% may result in a bonus of four years' salary.

Chapter 12: Conclusions

We have come to the end of our exploration into the world of sales. I hope that through our discussions, you have gained a comprehensive understanding of this field and its various aspects. Sales provide you with the opportunity to explore, analyze, categorize, and ultimately sell products or services.

Furthermore, this sales journey opens multiple avenues for generating income with each sale made.

A significant conclusion from this journey is that selling revolves around addressing the problems and needs of customers. The quicker you can identify and propose solutions to resolve these issues using your products and/or services, the more adept you will become as a salesperson.

This new role in consultative sales will offer you unique knowledge and experiences that cannot be obtained through any other position, allowing you to explore and develop within the business world in unparalleled ways.

Every business and company rely on sales as their primary and most important activity. By excelling in this new role, you will undoubtedly unlock new opportunities and open doors to success in any future professional endeavors you pursue.

Finally, I extend my best wishes for your success in your new sales role and welcome you wholeheartedly to the dynamic world of sales.

Figures

About the Author

The author has over 20 years of technical experience and has spent the past decade focused on consultative sales and projects.